finding things out

by
Rhona Arthur
Eion Johnston
Sheila McCullough

Chambers

CHAMBERS

An imprint of Chambers Harrap Publishers Ltd
7 Hopetoun Crescent
Edinburgh EH7 4AY

First published by Chambers Harrap Publishers Ltd 2007
© Scottish Library and Information Council 2007

A CIP catalogue record for this book is available from the British Library.

ISBN: 978 0550 10339 0

Series Editor: Ian Brookes
Editorial Assistance: Vicky Aldus, Sheila Ferguson
Prepress Controllers: Heather Macpherson, Becky Pickard

Designed and typeset by Chambers Harrap Publishers Ltd, Edinburgh
Printed and bound in Spain by GraphyCems

CONTENTS

Introduction

The term *information explosion* is used to describe the way in which the amount of available information is increasing at greater and greater rates. This process has been present for many years with more books, magazines as well as research papers being produced. But it has become more apparent to us all because of the almost universal availability of the Internet. Using the Internet to carry out a search for *information explosion* yields over thirty million results. If the search is restricted to these two words appearing in order and next to one another the results reduce to a 'reasonable' 270,000. However, if you spent only thirty seconds inspecting each of this reduced number of results, it would still take you nearly one hundred days working continually.

The rate at which the available information is increasing is so great that it is almost impossible to comprehend. So, searching for the right piece of information can be like hunting for a needle in a haystack. The term *information literacy* is used to describe the skill of finding the correct information and interpreting it correctly. Being information literate is like having the key which unlocks the door to finding facts.

You are reading this book because you have information needs. It could be finding a budget hotel in a holiday resort, tracking down a specialist supplier for a hobby, looking for the shortest route for a trip or searching for information to complete an assignment for your studies or work.

This book is designed to help you develop the skills which will save you time and reduce frustration when searching for information. The first section looks at the Information Task and shows you how to identify *keywords*, develop a strategy for searching and action planning. This is followed by sections which look at the three main types of information sources – paper, electronic and people. In each, we look at how information is organized and what you need to know to find what you need quickly.

It is not enough to simply find some information. How do you know if it is suitable? Unfortunately, information which is published on the Internet in particular may not be subject to any of the careful checks which a publisher carries out before investing in printing and marketing a book. As social networks grow and posting information on the Internet becomes easier, you need to be very careful about information you find on blogs, websites and wikis. We have included a section on how you can start to protect yourself from being misled by erroneous information by evaluating information methodically, treating it with caution.

Another problem facing you is safely re-using the information and keeping on the right side of the copyright laws. You will get some helpful guidelines to follow so that you attribute the source of your ideas clearly and can present assignments which are properly referenced. This might not seem important if your information task is not related to education. However, it is useful to learn how to record references so that you can return to information sources in future. For example, you may wish to find the website with the best offer or where you found the answer to the pub quiz and want to prove the quiz-master wrong.

The final section helps you review the process so that you can learn how to improve your technique for future information tasks. Throughout the book we have included examples which we hope you will find helpful and some exercises to try, making the job of developing information skills more enjoyable.

We know that searching for information can often be painstaking and frustrating. But there is real satisfaction to be found in designing your search so that you locate the information you need. This book will help you save time and allow you to tackle information tasks with confidence.

In search of information

Today's society is often referred to as the 'information society' and it is said that we live in the 'information age'. These expressions indicate that there is more information available in the twenty-first century than at any previous point in time. They also imply that in order to function effectively in the modern world, people require the skills to locate relevant and up-to-date information.

There are lots of times that we need to find information. Some examples would be finding information about:

- a college project topic
- a destination for a holiday you are taking
- features of a digital radio you are considering buying
- your family history
- setting up your own business
- health problems
- finance deals

These are examples which involve more effort than just looking at a single book or searching once on the Internet. In fact these are *information tasks*. To complete an information task successfully you have to carry out a number of steps:

- decide exactly what you are looking for
- think about how you will go about finding all the relevant information
- undertake the searching
- make sure that the information is reliable and exactly what you were seeking

Defining the task

The first step is to get a really good idea of exactly what information is being sought. It is necessary to define the task explicitly. Since this is the first activity upon which all the others depend, it is vital that this is absolutely clear from the start. The following aspects have to be decided:

- the precise topic involved
- the amount and level of information required
- the timescale for completion of the task
- the format and final form of the information

Defining the topic

The topic for the information task needs to be clearly defined. It needs to be expressed in words which describe it exactly. Then these words can be used later on in the searching.

For instance, if you were seeking information about feline leukaemia (a disease suffered by domestic cats), the terms 'animal illnesses' and 'cat diseases' are too vague to define your topic. If you were investigating the best account available for your savings, you would want to define which features of savings accounts were important to you – ease of access, term of investment, level of risk, and so on.

The amount and level of information

It is important to decide on the amount of information required for the information task. Too much information is just as bad as too little. Sifting out the required information from the mass of data available is one of the skills required in searching for information. On the other hand, a search may come up with very little information. Here the skill is in locating 'difficult-to-find' information.

Generally speaking, the more specific the topic of your search, the less information is likely to be available. Looking in an encyclopedia for information about domestic cats will undoubtedly yield more information than if you search only under one specific breed, such as Tonkinese cats.

Also, there is more likely to be information available on topics which are of interest to a large number of people. Fewer than 15 UK residents contract the bacterial disease brucellosis each year. So one might expect to find less information on this illness than on breast cancer, a high-profile condition where around 45,000 new cases are diagnosed each year.

You need to be clear about how much information you need. If you are thinking of buying shares in a certain company, you want to look at the recent performance of its shares and explore any political or economic factors which might cause the share price to go up or down. You can exclude any information relating to the company's activities from a historical perspective, biographies of its founders, etc.

Exercise

Think about the following information tasks. Would you require a little or a lot of information to answer the query?

1 buying a new house in Manchester

2 the symptoms of measles

3 current postage rates for letters and parcels

Check your answers on page 129.

The level of information required ranges from simple to complex. A decision must be made as to where in this range the task lies. Information at a complex level will use words and jargon not commonly understood by the general reader. A search for high-level information would be appropriate for someone who is an expert in the field (or at least a well-read amateur). Information for the general public must be at a much simpler level. You need to think about your own level of knowledge and expertise in the topic area to select an appropriate level for the information you will use.

Exercise

Think about the following information tasks. What level of information is required?

1 Finding out the best things to feed a pet guinea pig

2 Getting a description of the effect of atmospheric pressure changes on turbo chargers in high performance car engines

3 Establishing the procedures for objecting to a neighbour's planning application for an extension

Check your answers on page 129.

The timescale for completion

If you are carrying out the information task in connection with a study or work activity, it is important for your planning (and your stress levels!) that you are clear from the outset about the timescale. You will not produce a high-quality report or presentation if you have gathered the supporting information hurriedly a few days before the deadline.

Knowing how long you have to complete the task will help you to work out when you need to get started and how long you can afford to spend on each part of the task. It is important to remember that things can go wrong, and you should allow extra time for unforeseen problems.

The final form of the information

When an information task is being carried out in conjunction with study or work, the results will probably be put into one of the following formats:

* an essay
* a report
* a presentation
* an audio-visual product

Before starting to gather information on the topic, it is important to be clear about the format which the final product will take. This will affect the format of information which needs to be collected. For example, it is not possible to include audio information in an essay or report. In a PowerPoint® presentation, on the other hand, it is possible to include information in the form of writing, audio, still images and even moving images.

Example

You have to make a presentation to colleagues about population trends in Wales to help them predict sales figures. Here is how you might break down the information task:

• Topic definition: Trends in overall population and numbers of males and females in different age bands.

• Amount of information: Presentation is only 15 minutes, so restrict to population over the next 5 years and give only facts, without looking at the underlying reasons.

• Level of information: For people who are not experts in statistics.

• Format: For use in a PowerPoint® presentation with graphs.

Think for a moment about an information task you might carry out and how you could define it in a similar way.

Strategies for searching

The process of devising a search strategy can be split into four parts:

• choosing the keywords
• choosing the information sources
• deciding on the order of searching
• establishing a timetable

IN SEARCH OF INFORMATION

Choosing the keywords

Once the topic is precisely defined, it can then be expressed in *keywords*. These are carefully chosen words which fully express the meaning of the topic and can be used as search terms. We will discuss the idea of keywords more fully on pages 7–13.

When you are seeking information from a person, you can ask a fairly detailed question, knowing that they will get a good idea of what you are looking for. When you are using a paper source like an encyclopedia or an electronic source like a search engine, you are rather more restricted in the words that you can use. You need to use keywords to describe the topic of your search. You then look up these keywords in a printed index or type them into the search box on a website.

Choosing the information sources

Next it is necessary to choose the information sources. Deciding on the best sources of information for the topic is a key to success. The different types of source – paper, people and electronic sources – are covered in detail later in this book. However if you are in a library, you can always ask the librarian to suggest appropriate information sources. For some information tasks, it will be clear that one type of source – paper, say – will suffice. Other tasks may require the use of two or all three types of source to get information that is sufficiently detailed and precise.

Deciding on the order of searching

The third step is to decide on the order of searching. This means that, as well as thinking about which sources to use, it is important to consider what is the most logical order in which to examine them.

> **Example**
>
> You are carrying out an information task related to the development of women's rugby. You already know that one of your neighbours plays for her university women's rugby team and have decided that she would be a useful

people source. However, before you interview this lady, it would make sense to have gathered a good deal of background information on women's rugby from paper or electronic sources so that you can make best use of your time in the interview by asking the correct questions.

Establishing a timetable

For some simpler tasks you may be able to find all the information you require from one or more Internet sources. But for more complex searches it will be necessary to establish a timetable. You need to fit the searching in with the scheduling requirements of your information task and the activity which has prompted it.

> **Example**
>
> You are asked to produce a report on the products, services and prices offered by the major competitor firms to the company for which you work. This report will be printed and circulated to the company directors. Clearly this is an in-depth investigation which is likely to take some considerable time. It will be important to tackle it in a methodical way and to schedule enough time for gathering information before starting to write the report.

Keywords

On page six we mentioned the term 'keyword'. Before going further, it will be helpful to explain about keywords in more detail.

What is a keyword?

A keyword is a significant word in the description of a topic for which you are searching. It describes the topic fully or describes an important aspect of the topic.

Let's say your information task is *how you go about downloading classical music for an MP3-player*. This phrase has 10 words. The most significant of these are:

- downloading (the action you want to take)
- music (the material you want to download)
- classical (specifies what type of music you want)
- MP3-player (where the downloaded music is to be stored)

These would be useful keywords when searching for information on this topic.

In this example, the words 'how', 'you', 'go' and 'about' are not useful keywords because they do not add information to the keywords already chosen. Words like 'for' and 'an' are never useful keywords: their role in the topic description is to make it grammatically correct.

Keywords are usually nouns (*music*, *MP3-player*), verbs (*download*) or adjectives (*classical*).

Some practice at choosing keywords

Let's look at a couple of topics and see how we might choose keywords for searching.

Suppose your task is to find *the way you would cook turnips to go with haggis for a Burns Supper*. There are quite a few words here and choosing the best keywords is a bit more difficult.

Look at the phrase again, word by word:

- Is 'you' vital to the meaning?
- Is 'to' or 'go' or 'with' vital to the meaning?

We know that these short words have to be there for the sake of grammar, but the words that carry the most meaning are:

- the nouns 'turnips' and 'haggis'
- the verb 'cook'

Although there is information in the phrase 'for a Burns Supper', it is an additional reference-point for the activity. It may be that there is a special way of cooking turnip for a Burns supper, but that is probably a secondary issue.

There is no exact answer to finding the correct keywords. However here the really important words are 'cook' and 'turnip' and 'haggis'.

You can see that we can use words directly from the topic description as the keywords. This is a particularly useful technique when looking for keywords for use with electronic sources such as the Internet.

Another topic might be expressed as *effects on the environment of wind power versus coal-fired electricity power stations*. This is a more difficult description from which to select keywords because it contains a lot of meaningful words. All of the following have a bearing on the topic:

- effects
- environment
- wind power
- coal-fired
- electricity
- power stations

The number of keywords can be cut down by exploring the interaction between the various components in the topic description. The task is defined in terms of 'effects' of different power sources on the environment. All of the following are directly related to this:

- the **environment** is the thing being affected
- **wind** is one source which is doing the affecting
- **coal** is another source which is doing the affecting
- **electricity** is the reason why the process is undertaken

So the minimum set of keywords could be 'environment', 'wind', 'coal' and 'electricity'.

> _Exercise_
>
> What keywords would you use when searching for information to answer these questions?
>
> 1 What are the symptoms of measles?
>
> 2 What colour is the flower commonly known as cornflower?
>
> 3 Who is the Director-General of WHO (the World Health Organization)?
>
> Check your answers on page 130.

Choosing a single keyword

Sometimes a single word may be used instead of a group of words describing something. If the topic of interest is related to desks, chairs and bookshelves, the single keyword 'furniture' could be used. If the topic of interest related to bees, wasps and spiders, the more general keyword 'insect' could be substituted for the more specific names.

Although keywords are required when searching any type of information source, finding a single general keyword can be especially important in specific cases. For example if you are going to use a paper-based information source such as an encyclopedia, it may group topics in this way.

Using a single keyword also opens up the range of information which will be found. This can cause problems, increasing the volume of information obtained, some of which will be irrelevant. In using 'furniture' as a single keyword for information on desks, chairs and bookshelves (as above), you may also receive information about beds and sofas.

Synonyms

In the English language it is often the case that there is a range of words which can be used to describe essentially the same thing.

These are called *synonyms*. An example would be using the word 'canine' instead of 'dog'. Although synonyms might have slightly different meanings, they are used interchangeably.

Synonyms can cause a problem when searching electronic and paper sources. The keyword you choose may not be the same word that is used by the source, and the result may be that no information is found.

With indexes to paper sources, there are often (but not always) cross references between synonyms, as in '*Canine see Dog*'. So, with paper sources, if the keyword is not found in the index, it is usually worthwhile to explore synonyms for the keyword.

Electronic sources may not have the information stored under your choice of synonym and you will have to think of alternatives.

> *Exercise*
>
> **1** What are two synonyms for the word 'carpenter'?
>
> **2** What are two synonyms for the word 'mistake'?
>
> **3** What are two synonyms for the word 'poetry'?
>
> Check your answers on page 130.

Ambiguous words

It is important to remember that some words are *ambiguous* – that is, they have two or more meanings. For example, the word 'China' can mean a country in the Far East or a type of pottery. The English language is particularly rich in such ambiguities.

When searching an electronic source, it cannot know which particular meaning is intended when an ambiguous word is input. Try to be aware of such words so that you can use a non-ambiguous synonym.

Exercise

1 Give two possible meanings for the word 'cycle'.

2 Give two possible meanings for the word 'yarn'.

3 Give two possible meanings for the word 'kids'.

Check your answers on page 130.

When you are searching electronic sources, a possible solution to this problem is to add an additional word which clarifies the meaning. In the example of 'China', the inclusion of the word 'Beijing' as an additional keyword would result in information about the country China.

Using keywords in information searching

The importance of keywords may vary according to what type of source you are using in your information search.

People sources

When people are being used as a source of information, it is possible to use whole descriptive sentences and keywords do not have a great part to play. Clearly any descriptive sentence has to be thought out carefully to make sure that it expresses the topic area exactly. However, it does not need to be reduced to just a few or even one descriptive word. You will undoubtedly become involved in a discussion, during which any ambiguities about exactly what information you are seeking will be ironed out.

Paper sources

With a book, keywords need to be chosen and used to look up the index at the back of the book. It is sometimes not possible to use a group of descriptive keywords, you can only use one word (or sometimes a phrase) at a time. However in a well-indexed book you would find different aspects of the topic listed under the main heading, as in this example:

Often the paper-based information source will be a dictionary or encyclopedia. There is a choice of whether to look first for a general keyword or a more specific one. This will depend on:

- the type of information which is being searched for
- how good the index to the printed source is

It is particularly useful to think of a number of alternative keywords (synonyms), which then can be looked up individually.

Electronic sources
When using an electronic information source such as the Internet, you are able to group a number of keywords together to give a more exact description.

Evaluating the information

After you have completed your search and retrieved the information, it is necessary to evaluate it. This means deciding:

- whether it is really what you need
- whether it is really what it appears to be

In this way you can avoid using less useful or unreliable information.

Once you have retrieved several pieces of information you will be in a position to start deciding whether some part of your search strategy needs to be revised. A common problem is that quite a lot of the information you are retrieving does not quite match your topic area. You then need to revise your search strategy, looking especially at the keywords you have chosen and possibly at the information sources you are using.

Organizing your information search systematically in this way should

result in you having sufficient, reliable and relevant information for
your purposes.

Forming an action plan

In many cases it is very useful to have an action plan for the whole
information task. Forward planning means that all of the task
activities can be listed and fitted into a realistic schedule.

Why is planning necessary?

Planning your information task often helps you to save time.
When people feel enthusiastic about a new project or activity, the
temptation is always to leap in immediately and rush around doing
things which may not be the most useful activities in respect of
the project as a whole. This often results in crucial activities being
missed out, activities undertaken in the wrong order so that some
have to be repeated, and in the end there may not be enough time
to complete all the activities. Proper planning avoids these pitfalls.
The production of an action plan means thinking systematically
about the planning process.

The planning process

Planning involves thinking about:

- **Why** are you doing the task?
- **What** are you going to do?
- **How** are you going to do the task?
- **Which** resources do you require for the task?
- **Who** can help you?
- **Where** are you going to do the task?
- **When** are you going to do the task?

Asking the questions in this order gives a logical structure for the
planning process. The different tasks involved are often referred to
as the *stages* of the planning process. There is quite a lot to think
about here so take each of these stages in turn.

Think for a moment of an information task you might carry out yourself and keep it in mind while looking at each of the following aspects.

Why?

It is important to know why you are doing something! We saw at the start of this chapter that there are many reasons for undertaking an information task. It is worth listing a few of these again:

- a college project topic
- a destination for a holiday you are taking
- features of a digital radio you are considering buying
- your family history
- setting up your own business
- health problems
- finance deals

Think for a moment: Why do you wish to carry out the information task?

What?

Here you can record your searching objectives. But you need to be very clear in the details, giving:

- the precise topic involved
- the amount and level of information required
- the timescale for completion of the work
- the format and final form of the information

Think for a moment: Consider each of the four points above in relation to your information task.

How?

In order to search for information on your chosen topic you require a search strategy covering:

- a choice of keywords

- the choice of information sources (paper, people and electronic sources)
- the order in which you will search these information sources
- the evaluation of the information found

> **Take a moment** to write a short summary of a possible search strategy for your information task, covering the points above.

Which?

Think about the resources which you will need to carry out your search. These might include:

- IT equipment – a PC, printer, scanner, Internet connection, etc
- a photocopier
- transport in order to travel to libraries or to interview people sources
- stationery – a clipboard, markers, paper, folders
- audio-visual equipment – a mobile phone, a digital camera, a video camera

> **Take a moment** to list all the equipment which you will need for your information task.

Where?

Decide on the best locations to carry out your information task. Some activities will almost certainly be carried out in your home or workplace. But you may need to go further afield to access people or paper sources. If you do not have a computer with Internet access in your home or workplace, you may need to go to a local library or to a friend's house to access electronic sources.

> **Take a moment** to look at the activities in your search strategy and the resources required for these. What would be the best location for each activity?

When?

Work out a schedule that will allow you to complete your task comfortably before the finishing date. The following points need to be taken into account in order to create a useful schedule:

* Take the final finishing date for your activity and work back from there. How far before this date will you need to have completed your information task? For example, if your activity is an essay which will take you two weeks to write, then you will have to complete your information task two weeks before the essay submission date. If you plan to book a holiday in three weeks' time, you will need to carry out all your research on possible resorts, travel methods, prices, etc, before you actually make the booking.

* Look at the elements of your information task. How long is each likely to take?

* Can some only be carried out on certain dates (eg meeting a people source) or at certain times (eg within public library opening hours)?

* Do some depend on others being completed? (For example, you need to finish defining the keywords for the topic before you can start consulting an encyclopedia.)

* Do build in leeway to the timescale in case of problems, such as your computer network going down. Look carefully to see that your timings are realistic.

Once you have completed this last planning stage, you should have all the information required to produce an action plan for your information task.

What the action plan will look like

Now the answers to the above questions need to be organized into a chronological action plan.

Here is an example of the first part of such a plan for an information task related to a study activity:

IN SEARCH OF INFORMATION

Why	I am gathering information for the project which forms part of my college course on childcare.
What	My **topic** is *Introducing 3-4-year-old children to activities which encourage a co-operative and productive nursery environment.* I have to gather a sufficient amount of information to present a 10-minute talk to other students in my class, using PowerPoint® slides. So it would be useful to get information in text and pictorial **format.** The information needs to be at a **level** which both I and my fellow students will understand. I am doing my talk at the end of this term (10 weeks from now) – so I want to have all the information gathered in 6 weeks' time. That leaves me a couple of weeks to spare if I find I need more information or I find I don't get the information as quickly as I originally planned.

When	How	Which resource	Who	Where
Week 1 Tues pm	Choosing keywords	Paper and pen for note taking; Whiteboard	The lecturer, Mrs Logan; Brainstorming with classmates who are doing similar topics	Room 4B
Week 1 Thurs am	Start thinking about possible sources	Paper and pen for note taking	One of the college librarians	College learning resource centre

This is just one way of representing the action plan. You may think of other methods.

And remember, it is highly unlikely that everything will run smoothly according to your original action plan. You may find some excellent sources quite unexpectedly – but perhaps one of your 'people sources' will fall ill and not be able to meet with you at the scheduled time. So be flexible and keep amending your plan to take account of changing circumstances.

Information on paper

From earliest times human beings have had the urge to express themselves so that their ideas could be shared with others and preserved for posterity. Cave paintings have been found across the world dating from many thousands of years ago. Later, different civilizations used various media on which to record their ideas – clay tablets in Mesopotamia, wax tablets by the Romans, papyrus by the Egyptians, silk by the Chinese. From biblical times onwards, papyrus and parchment were preserved in rolls called scrolls – an early example of a sort of book.

A revolution in book production began in 1452 when Johannes Gutenberg invented the movable-type printing press. For the first time in history it became possible to produce books and other printed materials mechanically.

The impact of this at the time was at least as great as the impact of the Internet has been in recent years. With the printing press it was possible to produce multiple copies of books, leading to information becoming more widely available. This would allow the quicker spreading of new ideas. Initially it meant that moderately wealthy people could have a few books of their own. Eventually the cost of printing fell further, and by the 19th century even ordinary people could have their own copies of books.

Today there is wide access to printed information in a variety of formats. Printed materials can be bought from shops or websites. In addition, libraries make printed information available to the public.

Exercise

You may come across information on paper in various formats. Name the different formats from these descriptions:

1 A very common print information source, coming in all shapes and sizes. These items may contain stories or facts. They may be specially designed to convey information, as in the case of encyclopedias, dictionaries or atlases.

2 Publications which appear at regular intervals. They can be aimed at general or specialist readers and can include scholarly articles.

3 A paper information source which is intended to convey information to those looking at it. They are often fixed to walls. Although the information they contain is usually only valid for a short time, they can be useful sources for historical and social enquiries.

4 Usually very short printed items from a single page to perhaps ten pages long. They have a very focused purpose. They may convey information about an event happening locally. Longer versions might contain information about careers or health issues.

5 These printed sources and other original materials are useful for researching certain topics. They may form part of library collections and types include letters from famous people, documentary records from businesses, etc.

Check your answers on page 130.

Advantages of consulting paper sources

The obvious advantage of most paper information sources is their accessibility and portability. You do not require electrical equipment to read a book or newspaper and you can carry them anywhere and read them in a library, at home, or on public transport.

A second, perhaps less obvious, advantage of paper sources is that, because there is considerable effort and expense involved in producing them, they tend to be more reliable than some electronic sources. Nowadays almost anyone can produce web-based material for little or no cost. As a result, the content of many websites is either trivial or inaccurate. Books – certainly those produced by reputable publishers – tend to be more trustworthy because they have been through a process of selection, editing and proof-reading.

Disadvantages of consulting paper sources

The main disadvantage of using paper sources to find information lies in the difficulty of updating them. Publishers will print a certain number of copies of a book and the material will not be updated until a new edition is brought out, perhaps several years later. Many books are never updated at all.

Another major disadvantage of consulting a paper source is that it may be difficult to retrieve the information you want quickly. Electronic sources can have full-text indexing which allows you to search for any significant word in the text. Although paper sources may have indexes, even the most skilled of indexers will produce an index with a limited number of subject keywords.

And lastly, the sheer size of paper information sources presents challenges about how to store them. You can easily judge this by comparing the space required to store a 30-volume print encyclopedia with its equivalent on CD-ROM or DVD-ROM.

However, it should be recognized that paper sources still have an important part to play in the task of finding things out. The trick lies in recognizing when it will be quicker and easier to use paper sources rather than their electronic relations.

Books

Even in today's electronic, multimedia age, when the word 'library' is mentioned, the first image that comes into most people's minds is that of shelves of books. Although there is widespread access to information in electronic, multimedia formats, the printed book still has an important part to play when searching for information. In certain situations, books can be quicker, more reliable, more comprehensive and easier to use than electronic sources.

Books are usually divided into two main categories: fiction and non-fiction.

Fiction

Fiction is based on the imagination and not on actual facts or events. The most common sorts of fiction are novels and short stories. The usual intention of fiction writers is for their books to be read continuously, from cover to cover, rather than to be dipped into as sources of information. These books often have imaginative titles which give little clue as to the story line.

In libraries books containing fiction are usually arranged on the shelves alphabetically by the surname of the author. A fuller explanation of libraries and how to use them can be found on pages 51–2.

Non-fiction

Non-fiction deals with things that have happened or are happening. Books in this category might cover subjects such as geography, history, philosophy, politics, psychology, social studies or travel. Often, it may be appropriate just to look at one section which contains the specific information required rather than to read the whole book from cover to cover. Unlike fiction, the title of a non-fiction book usually gives a clear indication of what the book is about. For example, if you find a book called *The Complete Guide to Household Repairs*, you immediately have a clear idea about what information it contains.

In libraries non-fiction books are usually arranged using a numerical system which brings books on the same or similar topics together on the library shelves. This is explained in more detail on page 52.

Exercise

Decide which of these books are fiction and which are non-fiction:

1 *Harry Potter and the Half-Blood Prince* by J K Rowling

2 *Wintersmith* by Terry Pratchett

3 *How to Pass Higher Human Biology* by Harry Hoey, Tony Aitken and Rab Dickson

4 *To Kill a Mockingbird* by Harper Lee

5 *Tony Blair: Prime Minister* by John Rentoul

6 *How to Cook the Perfect...* by Marcus Wareing

Check your answers on page 130.

Uses of books in information searching

When we want to find something out, we generally turn to non-fiction books. However, you should not dismiss fiction completely as a source of information. If you want to get a feel for customs and manners in Regency England, for example, the historical novels of Georgette Heyer can provide good insights. Similarly, the books of John Steinbeck effectively describe the problems of the Depression in the United States in the 1920s. To use fiction in this way, you need to be well versed in the themes preferred by various authors.

Nevertheless, the books you are likely to use to find things out will overwhelmingly be non-fiction books. In particular, information searches often involve the category of non-fiction called 'reference books', which includes dictionaries, encyclopedias and atlases. A fuller explanation of these reference books and how to use them can be found on pages 27–42. It is, however, vital not to overlook the importance of other non-fiction books as a source of information.

These might be textbooks, biographies or any factual book on a relevant topic. It is useful to learn how to exploit these books when looking for information. Knowing what these books contain and how they are arranged will help you find information more easily.

Parts of a non-fiction book

Non-fiction books will usually include these features:

* the book's **title** somewhere on the outside cover, often describing both the type of book and the content, eg *Dictionary of Nuclear Physics*
* a **title page** giving information about the author, publisher and date of publication
* a **contents page** (sometimes given the name 'Table of Contents'), listing the chapters or main sections of the book
* an **index**, listing the topics covered in the book in alphabetical order and indicating the pages on which each topic is mentioned

Some non-fiction books also contain these features:

* an **introduction**, or **preface**, written by the book's author or another subject expert and giving a quick summary of the book's aims and coverage
* a **glossary**, listing specialist words used in the book in alphabetical order and explaining their meanings
* a **bibliography** (sometimes given the name 'Further References'), giving the names of other books, articles, websites, etc referred to in the book or which the author thinks may be of interest to readers
* **information about the author**, often shown on the back cover, which can give an indication of how well qualified the author is to write about the topic

INFORMATION ON PAPER

Exercise

Get hold of three or four non-fiction books and keep them at hand so that you can refer to them for illustrations of the points made in the remainder of this section.

The title page

The title page can give us some important information about the book and how useful it is likely to be. In some cases the information is spread over both sides of the page.

This shows you:

- the name of the author
- the title of the book
- the edition, which shows how many earlier versions of the book have been produced
- the publisher's name
- the date the book was published

Although these items are provided mainly for the purposes of identifying a particular book, they can also help you to evaluate the potential usefulness of the information contained within the book. If the author is an authority in their field, then the book is likely to contain useful information. For example, Delia Smith is a well-known expert in cookery, and so any book by her is likely to contain reliable information. The date of publication can be particularly significant if the subject is a fast-changing topic. For example, a book about space exploration published in the 1950s is not particularly useful for information tasks investigating later developments such as manned space flights or moon landings.

The contents page

As a minimum, the contents page should list all the chapters of the book, in the order in which they appear, together with the page number on which each chapter starts. Some contents pages also list any subsections into which the main chapters are divided.

Scanning down the contents page gives you a much better impression as to whether the book will be useful for your information task than the title can do by itself.

The index

The index is usually located at the back of the book, after the main text.

The index lists in alphabetical order the topics included in the book and the page or pages where information about these topics can be found. The index should lead you to the specific information you require.

Exercise

1 Which part of a non-fiction book gives you meanings of specialist words used in a book?

2 Where can you find information in a book about the publisher and copyright date of that book?

3 Where would you find information about the author's reason for writing a book?

Check your answers on page 131.

All of the parts of a book described here are included by the publishers to help readers. By making full use of them, it is possible to extract from any book all the information relevant to your search.

Dictionaries

Everyone is familiar with dictionaries. They are alphabetical lists of words, giving information about each word listed. It is worth noting that not all books providing information about the meanings of words actually have the word 'dictionary' in their title. Books with the words 'wordbook', 'glossary' or 'lexicon' in the title may also have useful information.

Although dictionaries are a type of book, they present information in a special way, and so it is worth considering them separately from other books. There are several types of dictionary and each has its own purpose.

English dictionaries

The type of dictionary you are most likely to use to find information is an English language dictionary. This can be used to:

- find the meaning of a word
- check the correct spelling or pronunciation of a word

Besides this basic information, larger dictionaries will provide these features:

- explanations of the origin of words
- examples or quotations illustrating the usage of a word
- related words and phrases

As well as answering your specific questions about a word, dictionaries can be used to check the meaning or spelling of a keyword which has been selected for an information search.

Example:

Here is a typical example of the entry in a dictionary for the word 'educate':

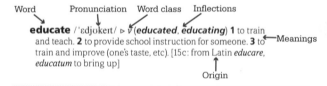

Besides the meanings of the word, the dictionary also gives information about the way a word is pronounced, the word class to which it belongs, the different forms of the word (known as 'inflections') and the origin of the word. Notice that the dictionary uses certain standard symbols and abbreviations to pack the information into a relatively short space: the pronunciation of the word is shown using the International Phonetic Alphabet, and the abbreviation 'v' stands for 'verb'. A dictionary should have a key to the meanings of symbols and abbreviations. This is often found at the front of the book, but sometimes there is also a key at the foot of each page.

> *Exercise*
>
> Look up the word 'educate' in another English dictionary. Compare the information given there with our example.

The English language changes rapidly. New words are being added all the time and older words fall out of use. There will not be any definition of the word 'Internet' in a dictionary published in the 1970s. So, if you need to find the meanings of up-to-date concepts it is best to use a dictionary which is no more than a few years old.

There are many different English dictionaries, ranging from small pocket versions with only a limited selection of words and minimal information on each word to the multi-volume *Oxford English Dictionary* which is the most comprehensive and authoritative dictionary of English. The important point is to choose the right size of dictionary which matches the complexity of your search. There is no need to plough through a multi-volume dictionary when checking the spelling of a fairly common word, but a very small dictionary may not include all the information you need.

Another point to remember when using dictionaries is that British English and American English often differ in both spelling and meaning. For example, the word spelt 'honour' in the UK is spelt 'honor' in the USA. The luggage compartment of a car is called the 'boot' in the UK and the 'trunk' in the USA. So if you are looking to find the correct British spelling and usage, you should make sure you are using a dictionary published in the UK.

Bilingual dictionaries

'Bilingual' or 'translating' dictionaries do not give the meaning of the word but its equivalent in another language. Usually they are in two parts: one giving translations from language A to language B, and the other giving translations from language B to language A. As with English dictionaries, bilingual dictionaries commonly give an indication of pronunciation and word class. Sometimes, with languages which have more complicated grammar than English they will give additional grammatical information, such as whether the noun is masculine, feminine or neuter or how to make different tenses of a verb.

Here is an example from an English–German dictionary:

chewing gum [*tchu-ing gum*] n, Kaugummi (m)

The English word 'chewing gum' is given along with its pronunciation and then the equivalent German word 'Kaugummi'. The letter 'm' that appears in brackets indicates that the German noun is masculine.

Subject dictionaries

Subject dictionaries focus on the specialized words used in particular subject areas. They are particularly useful in subjects such as science and technology. In libraries, these are usually placed beside the books on the topic concerned rather than in the separate reference section.

Exercise

Have a look in your library and see which subject dictionaries, you can find. Think how you might be able to use any of these to assist with an information task.

Special-purpose dictionaries

Another type of dictionary is the special-purpose dictionary that is produced to meet some particular need. For example, dictionaries of abbreviations explain the full meaning of abbreviations and acronyms, while dictionaries of quotations can be used to find who said or wrote something or to complete a half-remembered phrase or saying. Dictionaries of names explain the meaning and derivation of forenames and surnames. These are particularly popular with parents expecting a baby but are also of interest to people exploring the origin of their own name.

Dictionaries in electronic format

With dictionaries it is often quicker to consult the print version rather than search electronically. If you have an English–Spanish dictionary on your desk and want to know the meaning of a Spanish word, it will probably be faster to look the word up in the book than find a suitable website and type in the word. However, you may not have to hand a particular printed dictionary which is suitable for your enquiry, and in such a case you will find a wealth of web-based dictionary resources to provide the information you require.

Unlike a book, where all the words can be seen when the pages are open, none of the words can be seen when a web-based dictionary is opened. Instead a search box is displayed on the screen for users to enter the word or phrase they want. One disadvantage of this 'type in the box' method is that you cannot scan down a column of words as you can with a printed dictionary.

Exercise

Look up the word 'educate' in these online dictionaries and compare the results.

http://dictionary.cambridge.org

http://www1.oup.co.uk/elt/oald

http://www.yourdictionary.com

Because so much of the material on the Internet originates in the USA, it is important to be aware of the differences between British and American English when using electronic dictionaries.

Encyclopedias

Encyclopedias have been a popular source of information since the 18th century. (It is worth noting that the traditional spelling of this word is 'encyclopaedia', with an extra 'a', but the spelling 'encyclopedia' is now more widely used.) These books come in various sizes: some are single volumes, but others may consist of as many as 30 volumes. They contain articles giving information on all sorts of things including people, places, events and ideas. The articles are listed in alphabetical order by the subject.

Encyclopedias are available for a range of reading ages and levels from children to adults and can be found in different languages.

Encyclopedias are produced in both printed and electronic formats. The electronic formats can be disk-based or available online via the Internet. The disk-based versions of encyclopedias are either on CD-ROM or DVD-ROM. The DVD-ROM disks are ideal for large encyclopedias as they can hold nearly ten times as much information as a CD-ROM. Most of the well-known encyclopedias also appear in frequently-updated online versions, access to which is restricted to those who have paid a subscription fee.

General encyclopedias

General encyclopedias like *Encyclopaedia Britannica* or the *World Book Encyclopedia* are multi-volume encyclopedias and contain information on a wide range of topics, attempting to cover the whole of human knowledge. Each subject is covered by one or more articles which are generally written by subject experts.

It is, however, important to remember that the information contained within any encyclopedia may have a particular emphasis because of the background of the subject experts or the publishers. For instance, the *World Book Encyclopedia* is published in the United States and is not a particularly helpful source of information on the details of UK government. It is useful to be aware of this possibility and evaluate the information as you would from any information source.

Subject encyclopedias

Practically every subject area now has its own encyclopedia, some as single volumes, some as multiple volumes. Sometimes the single volumes do not have the word encyclopedia in their title, but many books that include the words 'companion' or 'handbook' in their title are really subject encyclopedias, as too are some books that go under the misleading name of 'dictionary'.

A book called *The Encyclopedia of Scotland* would be helpful for finding out about topics such as the Highland Clearances, the Gaelic language, the whisky industry, Hogmanay or John Knox.

Subject-specific encyclopedias are available for a wide range of subjects from health and the sciences to art and gardening.

Exercise

Have a look in your library and find out which general and subject encyclopedias are there for your use. Remember to check for encyclopedias available in other formats such as CD-ROM or online.

Uses of encyclopedias

An encyclopedia is useful both for finding out general information on a wide range of subjects and specific information on one or more aspects of one subject.

It looks at the who, what, when, where, how and why of things so can answer individual questions such as:

* What size is a football pitch?
* How does a car work?
* Who invented the light bulb?

Example

The *World Book Encyclopedia* is a multi-volume encyclopedia found in many libraries. Volumes 1–21 contain the alphabetically listed articles; Volume 22 contains the Research Guide and Index.

At the top of each page there are guide words indicating which stretch of the alphabet is covered on that page.

The articles vary in length. Some are brief whilst others cover subjects in great depth. Typically an article has:

• an outline

• the information on the subject

- a photograph or other image of the subject

- questions to help you review information in the article

- a bibliography (a list of publications and their authors who have written on the subject)

Exercise

Find the 'Niagara Falls' article in the encyclopedia you have access to. Look at the layout and compare it to that given above.

Using a print encyclopedia

All encyclopedias that exist in printed form have detailed indexes to help you find information. The index is often contained in a separate volume from the articles. When using a print index, you will find it necessary to follow up cross-references and think of different keywords.

Example

If you needed to do some research on Georges Braque, the French artist, you might begin by looking for an encyclopedia entry under his name. But you might also find useful materials in an encyclopedia under 'Cubism' or 'French painting'.

There is more information about using indexes on pages 56–60.

Using an electronic encyclopedia

Encyclopedias in electronic format contain the same information as the printed versions. However, in addition to words and illustrations, electronic encyclopedias can also offer multimedia information such as moving pictures and sound. As the information is in electronic format, it is very flexible and easy to search using the alphabetical index (or listing) or by combining keywords.

Most of the well-established encyclopedias are available through the

Internet only on a subscription basis. You need to pay a fee before you can access the complete version, but you may be able to access these if a local library is a subscriber. Moreover, many encyclopedias offer cut-down versions free of charge. These abbreviated versions can still provide useful information.

These links give free access to restricted versions of two popular encyclopedias:

http://www.britannica.com

http://encarta.msn.com

Browsing through these will give an impression of how the full versions work.

> *Exercise*
>
> Find out which encyclopedias are available on CD-ROM or DVD-ROM in your library and which online encyclopedias your library subscribes to. Choose a subject such as 'The Industrial Revolution' and compare the information found in a print encyclopedia with that in the electronic encyclopedia.

Maps

At its simplest, a map is a graphical representation of an area of the earth. A map is normally printed or displayed with North at the top of the page. Maps can be used in information tasks such as the following:

* locating a particular city, town or village
* finding out which countries a particular river flows through
* working out directions to an address
* finding the distance between two places

So a map of the UK might show:

* the positions of the main cities: Belfast, Birmingham, Bristol, Cardiff, Edinburgh, Glasgow, Leeds, London, Liverpool, Manchester and Newcastle

- the locations of mountains
- the shapes of lakes

There are many different types of map:

- A **physical map** emphasizes the physical features such as hills, rivers and lakes, using different colours to represent the height of the land.
- A **political map** emphasizes the boundaries between countries and regions, as well as showing capital cities and major centres of population. There is normally no detail about mountains and hills.
- A **thematic map** gives statistical or other information in connection with the land areas shown on the map, for example population density, climate, natural resources or land use.
- A **road map** shows the motorways and main roads as well as likely destinations such as cities, towns, airports, ferry terminals and leisure destinations.
- A **detailed map** (such as those published by the Ordnance Survey) gives precise information on heights of the landscape and detail down to streets and individual buildings.

Map symbols

Symbols are used to show man-made features of the landscape, such as castles, electricity pylon lines or footpaths. There are variations in the symbols used, although different publishers often use similar symbols for some features, for example using a cross to represent a church. Each map will have a key explaining the meanings of the symbols that it uses.

Exercise

Find an Ordnance Survey map or look at one in the library and find which symbols represent the following:

1 a caravan site

2 a windmill

3 a castle

4 a coniferous wood

Check your answers on page 131.

Contour lines

Contour lines are used on maps to show heights and gradients. A contour line joins points which are all at the same height above sea level. The closer together the contour lines are in a particular place, the steeper the slope of the ground is. Contour lines are always shown on Ordnance Survey maps.

Exercise

Choose an Ordnance Survey map of your own area. Look for the contour lines and work out the height of the land around your own house.

Grid lines

Grid lines marked on each map are used to locate a particular feature or place. Many maps include an alphabetically arranged list of features and places. Each of these is listed with its grid reference. You can then use the grid references to find the locations on the map.

This is especially useful with street maps of cities, as well as finding towns on road maps.

The National Grid

The Ordnance Survey is the official producer of maps for Great Britain and Northern Ireland. It publishes several series of maps in different scales, ranging from a map with the whole country on one sheet to maps for professional surveyors that show individual buildings.

Ordnance Survey maps use a grid system which is specially designed to cover the whole of Great Britain. This is called the National Grid.

INFORMATION ON PAPER

In this system, the United Kingdom is divided up into a grid of 100 kilometre squares, each of which has been allocated a two-letter reference: for example, London is in area TQ. Each 100-kilometre square is then divided into 10-kilometre quares. The grid lines, marking each distance of 10km, are numbered 0–9, working from 0 in the south-west corner, to 9 in a northerly and easterly direction.

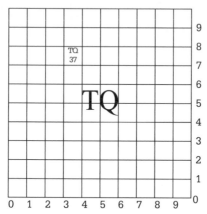

In more detailed maps, each of these 10 x 10 kilometre squares is further divided into 1 x 1 kilometre squares. Square TQ37 is shown on page 39.

A grid reference for the point marked 'x' on the map would look like this: TQ 305744. The first three numbers are horizontal co-ordinates, reading eastwards $^5/_{10}$ of a square from grid line 30; the second three numbers are vertical co-ordinates, reading northwards $^4/_{10}$ of a square from grid line 74.

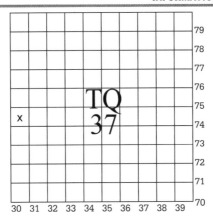

The National Grid offers a very simple method of giving a precise reference for any point in the country. As such it can be used both for leisure purposes (such as giving directions for orienteering) and more serious activities (such as mountain rescue).

Scale

The scale of a map states the ratio between the distance measured on the map and the actual distance as measured on the ground.

This table shows some commonly used map scales:

Scale	Typical use
1:10,000,000	Maps of continents
1:1,000,000	Maps of countries
1: 500,000	Maps of regions
1: 250,000	Large-scale local-area maps
1: 50,000	Detailed local-area maps

INFORMATION ON PAPER

Scale	Typical use
1: 20,000	Street maps
1: 1,250	Plans of individual buildings

A scale of 1:10,000,000 means that 1 centimetre on the map represents 10,000,000 centimetres (ie 100 kilometres) on the ground. So the larger the figure on the right-hand side of the ratio, the bigger the area the map covers and the less detail it will show.

Maps on the Web

For centuries, maps have been printed on large pieces of paper making them difficult to store. After the start of the electronic information revolution, publishers were quick to realize that their maps could be produced in digital format. This initially meant putting them on CD- ROMs. Nowadays, however, there are all sorts of maps available through the Web, including Multimap, Streetmap and Google maps. These electronic maps are easy to search and use. Of course, if you are going for a hike, you will prefer an old-fashioned folding map which can be packed into your bag.

> *Exercise*
>
> Have a look at each of these three Web map sites and decide what you might best use them for:
>
> http://www.multimap.com
>
> http://www.streetmap.co.uk
>
> http://maps.google.co.uk

Atlases

Atlases are basically collections of maps bound together with an index to the places shown on the maps. An atlas may comprise maps of a country, a continent or the whole world. A good index is vital so that the user can find the page with the correct map and the location of the desired place or feature on this map. The pages are numbered and the location on any page will be indicated using grid lines.

Printed atlases are used less frequently nowadays as it is often more convenient to seek the information from a web-based mapping service. However, large atlases such as the *Times Atlas of the World* can still be found in libraries. Moreover, the large detailed map pages of a printed atlas are easier to use for some purposes than what can be shown on a computer screen.

Road atlases are a special category of atlas. Most motorists have one of these in their car. They show roads in some detail and often highlight useful features such as motorway service stations or tollbridges. Here again, these printed sources are being superseded by printouts from online electronic map websites or by electronic satellite navigation systems (often known as 'satnav') in vehicles.

Gazetteers

Gazetteers are basically geographical dictionaries or geographical encyclopedias. They feature the names of places – cities, towns and villages – and physical features such as rivers or mountains. Basic information is given for each place or feature. For example, for a town the information listed might include its map reference, population, main industries and points of interest for a visitor. Nowadays few gazetteers are produced in printed format. However, old gazetteers are a useful source of historical information.

Exercise

Look at each of the three web-based gazetteers and decide what you could use each for:

http://www.geo.ed.ac.uk/scotgaz/scotland.html

http://www.gazetteer.co.uk

http://www.world-gazetteer.com

Changing geographical information

Geographical information changes frequently. So with maps and atlases it is very important to use up-to-date versions. The names and boundaries of countries alter to reflect political changes. For instance, in 1993 Czechoslovakia became two countries – the Czech Republic and Slovakia. Another way that geographical information changes is that names that were given to places by European explorers and colonizers are increasingly changed to a name which better reflects what the place is called by the inhabitants of the country, as with the case of 'Bombay' becoming 'Mumbai'.

Pamphlets

Pamphlets are small, unbound works on topics of current concern. The length of pamphlets varies and some might only consist of a single sheet. Information contained in pamphlets changes in depth, subject matter and reliability.

Historically, pamphlets were used to convey religious and political views and there are still large collections in libraries which may be useful for research. In recent times, pamphlets often take the form of single-sheet 'flyers' handed out in the street or inserted in newspapers, and many carry little value. Examples of pamphlets which might have greater value include advertising for arts performances, political electioneering information and health information distributed following vaccinations.

Newspapers

A newspaper is a paper-based publication, usually appearing daily or weekly. Newspapers are an important source of current information. Back copies of newspapers give information on events and attitudes from the past. All of the above should go without saying, but it is worth thinking a little more deeply when considering the value of newspapers as sources of information.

Think of any newspaper with which you are familiar, or look at a daily newspaper in your library. What sort of information does it contain?

Newspapers generally contain:

- news stories about local, national or international issues, including politics, education, leisure, business and sports
- in-depth 'feature' articles on the arts, fashion, health, motoring, etc
- comments and opinions, including letters from readers, leader articles or an 'editorial' which expresses the views of the editor, editorial team or publisher
- entertainments listings giving information about what is on television and radio, and events at cinemas, theatres and other venues
- puzzles and quizzes, such as crosswords and sudoku
- announcements of births, deaths and marriages
- weather forecasts
- advertisements, including large, display advertisements from retailers, classified advertisements from individuals looking to sell or buy items such as cars or furniture
- job advertisements, and advertisements of houses for sale or rent

Categories of newspapers

Newspapers have traditionally fallen into two categories: broadsheet and tabloid (the latter is sometimes also called 'red-top'). These terms were coined to describe the actual size and appearance of the pages in the newspaper. Tabloid pages are about half the area of broadsheet pages and tabloid papers have traditionally included more pictures and less written text. However, a recent trend is for the papers previously published in broadsheet size to adopt either tabloid-sized pages or an in-between size called Berliner. The terms 'broadsheet' and 'tabloid' are still used, but nowadays they differentiate between the more serious newspapers with lots of news coverage and the more frivolous ones which carry less 'hard' news.

The differences between the two styles can be summarized as follows:

INFORMATION ON PAPER

Tabloid newspapers	Broadsheet newspapers
an interest in personalities and celebrities, with little coverage of international events, except for major international tragedies	more coverage of political, financial and international news, with little coverage of celebrity gossip
shorter stories which are more easily read	more in-depth coverage of stories using more complex vocabulary and grammar
more and larger pictures	more text and fewer pictures
a more informal style	a more serious style
a more personal and emotive viewpoint, looking for the human interest in stories	a more analytical and dispassionate viewpoint, leaving readers to judge for themselves about major issues

> *Exercise*
>
> Decide which of these newspapers could be categorized as tabloids and which as broadsheets: *The Sun*, *The Guardian*, *The Daily Telegraph*, *The Daily Express*, *The Daily Mail*, *The Independent*, *The Daily Mirror*.
>
> Check your answers on page 131.

If you are not sure about any of these, look at a copy – a range will be available in your library.

Both broadsheets and tabloids have their uses when looking for information. If asked to investigate attitudes to women in the workplace in the 1970s, you would get detailed factual information on equal-opportunities legislation in broadsheets. The tabloids would provide insights on popular attitudes to women's issues.

Local and national newspapers

Newspapers can also be divided into local and national papers. All of the newspapers mentioned above are national papers. For information on local topics such as events in the Welsh Assembly, house prices in Newcastle or education in Northern Ireland you would be better to search in a regional paper such as *The Western Mail*, *The Northern Echo* or *The Belfast Telegraph*.

Readership and viewpoints

Each newspaper is owned by a particular person or organization. In some cases the owner will have a big say in the way in which news is reported. All newspapers have an editor who is responsible for implementing what is reported and how it is reported.

This means that many newspapers tend to promote a particular political viewpoint. *The Guardian* is generally accepted as giving a left-wing interpretation of events, whereas *The Daily Telegraph* is seen as politically right-wing. The result is that newspapers target particular types of readers.

The political stance of a newspaper will be reflected in:

* the choice of news items which are given prominence
* the tone and content of editorial articles
* letters from readers (who generally prefer a paper which reflects their own views)

When assessing the value of information in newspapers it is important to be aware of bias of any sort. This is especially important with regard to emotive topics such as immigration or crime and punishment.

Exercise

Obtain copies of *The Guardian* and *The Daily Telegraph* and compare the approach and treatment of these two papers to the major news stories of the day. Look at both the articles, the editorials and any pages written by columnists.

Newspapers in electronic format

When we use the word newspaper, we tend to have the image of the printed paper which is bought from a shop, delivered to the home or read in a library. Back copies of printed papers are extremely difficult to preserve, store and index. So newspaper publishers were quick to embrace the benefits of new technology by first archiving their papers onto CD-ROMs and making them accessible via the Internet. CD-ROM and Internet versions are not always identical to the printed copies. However, they are immensely useful when seeking information because of the search facilities which the electronic format offers.

> *Exercise*
>
> Look at the printed copy of any newspaper available in your library and compare it with the online version. Here are the websites of a few newspapers which you could use:
>
> http://www.express.co.uk
>
> http://www.dailymail.co.uk
>
> http://www.telegraph.co.uk
>
> http://www.independent.co.uk

Journals

The word 'journal' is used to cover all periodicals other than newspapers. Journals may be published weekly, monthly, or in some cases only a few times per year. There are many types of journals available including:

* popular magazines written for the general public, such as *Your Health* and *Cosmopolitan*
* publications aimed at readers with specific interests, such as *Photography Monthly* and *Practical Computing*
* trade journals written by and for people who work in specific professions, such as *Caterer & Hotel Keeper* and *Nursery World*

- academic journals written by and for people that are involved in research work within an academic or professional environment, such as the *British Medical Journal* and *Critical Quarterly*

Exercise

Look at the journals in your library and try to fit them into the four categories listed above. There may be none in the last category.

Most journals contain a mixture of articles containing news and up-to-date information on items such as new products, materials, projects, experiments and research. However, the wide range of journals means that the style and content can vary enormously. General-interest magazines may contain many glossy photographs and have an easy reading style, whereas academic journals tend to be serious, sober-looking publications with long articles and few or no pictures.

How do journals help in information searching?

Journals are most commonly used for:

- finding up-to-date information on specific topics or areas of interest
- keeping up to date with the latest developments in a subject
- looking for job vacancies or training opportunities
- finding detailed information about topics being researched

Most journals follow a similar layout. There is a contents page at the front listing the articles and features in that issue together with the page numbers where these articles can be found.

Online journals

The versions of most journals available on the Internet do not contain the full content of the printed issues, except where online subscription versions are offered. It is interesting to compare the online and printed versions of popular magazines.

Exercise

Look at the printed copy of a journal available in your library and compare it with the online version. Here are the websites of a few journals which you could use:

http://www.hi-fiworld.co.uk (*Hi-Fi World*)

http://www.private-eye.co.uk (*Private Eye*)

http://www.economist.com (*The Economist*)

http://www.whatcar.com (*What Car*)

http://www.marieclaire.co.uk (*Marie Claire*)

Finding things out from paper sources

We saw in the previous chapter that there are many different types of paper information source that can be used for information searching:

* books
* dictionaries
* encyclopedias
* atlases
* maps
* newspapers
* pamphlets
* magazines and journals

This list consists solely of published material. During an information search you may also consult items which have not been published but are original documents such as letters or notes of meetings.

How paper sources are arranged

Paper sources are usually arranged in a way that helps you find the information within them. However, the different types of paper source require different approaches.

Books have a title page, contents and index to help you find what you need. Full information about the layout of books is contained on pages 25–7.

Dictionaries and many encyclopedias have their contents arranged in alphabetical order. This means that you can use the keywords you have chosen for your information task and look for them directly in the dictionary or volume.

For most other paper sources, however, the main method of locating information is to use some form of index. An index is an alphabetical list of important words along with the page numbers(s) where they are mentioned in the paper source. This also applies to maps and atlases, where the alphabetical listing will be of geographical places.

Some reference books also include a special section at the front of the book – often with a title such as *How to use this book* – which gives useful tips on searching for information.

Journals and magazines usually have a contents page near the front of each issue. Many produce an index once a year to all the issues published in the preceding twelve months.

Make sure that you use all of these routes to get all the information you need. Taking a few minutes to familiarize yourself with a paper source and how it is organized will save time in the long run.

If at first you don't succeed...

Sometimes paper sources are not thoroughly indexed. If you look up a keyword and find that it is not listed, it does not necessarily mean that the book will not contain useful information. It may be worthwhile to think of alternative keywords to look up in the index and see if these lead you to the information you are looking for.

Exercise

1 If you want information on 'boats' and this word does not appear in the index, which alternative words might you try?

2 If you want information on 'boats' and this word does not appear in the index, which more general terms might you try?

Check your answers on page 131.

Keep a record of the details

Depending on the nature of your information task, it may be important to record the details of the paper source in which you found the information. References are especially important in educational information tasks. This is because you may need to go back to the paper source to check your information or to find out additional information. So it is important to note down the details so that you can find it quickly again.

Libraries

It is likely that most of the paper sources you will use in your information task will be found in a library, probably your local public library or possibly your school, college, university or workplace library.

Libraries organize their resources in broadly similar ways so that it is easy for people to find what they are interested in. General fiction is organized in alphabetical order by the author's surname. Popular genres or types of fiction such as crime and romance are organized in the same way but all of the books within the genre are kept together. Non-fiction books are arranged by a 'classification system' which organizes the books by subject. Resources in special formats, such as large-print books and DVDs, will be in separate sections, and there will usually be a separate reference section, with dictionaries, atlases, and so on.

To find out all the resources a library holds, you can use the library catalogue which, almost certainly, will be held on a computer. If you are not sure how the catalogue works, library staff will be able to assist you.

Exercise

Many libraries allow access to their computer catalogues online. Try a search for a subject which interests you using these catalogues:

http://librarycatalogue.leedslearning.net/TalisPrism
(Leeds Library and Information Service)

http://cairns.lib.strath.ac.uk (libraries of the Scottish
universities and some Scottish public libraries)

Using a library

Once you have used the catalogue to find a useful book or other
paper source, the next task is to find this source on the library
shelves. Most (but not all) libraries arrange their stock using the
Dewey Decimal System. This system divides knowledge into ten
broad subject areas and then subdivides these further into more
specific subjects. The aim of this classification system is to bring
together in the same place on the shelves items on the same topic
or on related topics.

For example, one of the ten sections is 'Natural Science and
Mathematics'. All topics that fall within this field have a number
between 500 and 599. But within this area the numbers from 520 to
529 are reserved for books about astronomy. And within the field of
astronomy, each topic has a particular number, so that books about
the planet Venus can be found at the specific number 523.42.

A librarian can explain the classification system more fully.

Some university and workplace libraries and a very few public
libraries arrange their stock using a different system called the
Library of Congress system. Again the library staff will be able to
explain to you how this works.

Alphabetization

When we go about finding information we are often faced with items
in alphabetical order. This may be the case when you look at indexes
in books and journals, when you search for articles in an encyclopedia,
or when you are trying to find a name in a telephone directory. Even
on websites, lists of topics are often arranged alphabetically.

Most people are familiar with the order of the letters in the alphabet and it is fairly easy to put a list of words into alphabetical order. Similar words have to be sorted carefully, applying the alphabet letter by letter through the words.

However, problems arise when the items listed consist of more than one word or include numbers or abbreviations.

The following sections cover these aspects and will help with the quick and efficient use of alphabetical indexes and lists.

Spaces

Alphabetical order would be very simple if all the terms being ordered consisted of only one word. However many terms will consist of two or more words. So the question arises: how are spaces dealt with? There are two methods, called the 'letter-by-letter' and 'word-by-word' systems.

In the letter-by-letter system, only letters are considered – spaces are ignored. In the word-by-word system spaces are given precedence and come before letters.

This is easier to understand by looking at an example. Here is the same list of words filed by both systems:

Letter by letter	*Word by word*
Newark	New England
New England	New Jersey
Newington	New Orleans
New Jersey	New York
New Orleans	Newark
Newtown	Newington
New York	Newtown

> *Exercise*
>
> 1 Arrange the items Easton, East Anglia, East Longtown, Eastleigh, Eastabington in alphabetical order using the word-by-word system
>
> 2 Arrange the same items in alphabetical order using the letter-by-letter system
>
> Check your answers on page 131.

The word-by-word system is most common in print information sources. Lists generated electronically tend to favour letter-by-letter. It is possible to tell which method has been used by looking closely at a list. If the item sought in an alphabetical list is not found where expected using one system, look for it in the place where it would occur with the other system.

Abbreviations

Another question relating to alphabetical order is how to treat abbreviations. The usual method is that abbreviations are ordered as if they were written out in full, so that 'Oxford Rd' is listed as if it were written 'Oxford Road'.

> *Exercise*
>
> List the following items in alphabetical order: Ashton St, Ashton Secondary School, Ashton Rd, Ashton Rowing Club, Ashton Railway, Ashton Stonemasons
>
> Check your answers on page 131.

Remember abbreviations may come at the beginning of the item rather than at the end. 'Dr' might stand for 'Drive' at the end of a street name, but it can also stand for 'Doctor', as in 'Dr MacNab'. 'St' stands for 'Street', but at the start of a name it can stand for 'Saint', as in 'St Peter'.

But the same rule applies in all cases: look for abbreviations as if they were written out in full.

Numbers

Just as with spaces, there are two methods for dealing with numbers. Either numbers are always listed before letters, or numbers are treated as abbreviations and listed as if they were words, for example '2' being listed as if it were spelt out as 'two'. Listing numbers before letters is by far the most common method.

Here is the same list of words filed by both systems:

Numbers before letters	*Numbers listed as words*
2 for tea	Tangerine
Tangerine	Tea at the hotel
Tea at 12	Tea at 12
Tea at the hotel	Tea at two
Tea at two	2 for tea
Two teas for us	Two teas for us

Exercise

List the following items in alphabetical order according to the two methods above: 7 Up , Seven Brides for Seven Brothers, Seventy-six Trombones, 7 o'clock, Seven times seven, 76 Arran Road

Check your answers on page 132.

Practical application

Knowing about these different systems should help you in finding what you are looking for in an alphabetical list. You may also find yourself compiling an alphabetical list as part of your information task. In that case, it does not usually matter which system you use for your alphabetical ordering so long as you are consistent. Use either the letter-by-letter or word-by-word method – but do not use a mixture of both.

Indexes

Indexes are found in many different paper information sources. They may be found in non-fiction books, in encyclopedias, in atlases and in collections of journals. The purpose of an index is to enable information to be retrieved quickly and easily when it is wanted.

An index is simply an alphabetical list of the topics contained in the source. For each topic the index gives a reference or references to show where information on that topic may be found.

Exercise

Choose a non-fiction book and find its index. Is it at the back? Keep the book beside you to refer to as you look at the following sections.

Book indexes

An entry in an index to a book may well have listings like this:

Education
Further education	*26, 55–57*
Primary schools	*24, 58–62*
Secondary schools	*25, 63–74, 97*
Universities	*27, 87–91*

The numbers that appear after the different items are the numbers of the pages in the book where the topics are covered. So the topic *Primary schools* is mentioned on page 24 and again between pages 58 and 62. It is likely that the longer section covers the topic in more detail.

Exercise

Look at the index of your chosen book. Find some examples of listings where single pages are given and where a set of pages is given. Do these latter examples explain the indexed word in more detail?

Encyclopedia indexes

A typical entry in an index to a multi-volume encyclopedia looks something like this:

Brazil **2** *15–22,* **7** *121, 124,* **14** *291,* **18** *312–314*

This indicates that information on Brazil is found in various articles. The bold number indicates the volume of the encyclopedia in which information is found, and this volume number is followed by the page numbers within that volume. In our example the information on Brazil is found in four articles:

- in Volume 2, pages 15 to 22, there is the main article, entitled 'Brazil'
- in Volume 7, pages 121 and 124, the Brazilian football team is featured in an article entitled 'Football'
- in Volume 14, page 291, information on Brazil Nuts is mentioned in an article entitled 'Nuts'
- in Volume 18, pages 312 to 314, some information about Brazil is included in an article entitled 'South America'

The Brazil example shows how important it is to use an index in order to locate *all* the information about a topic. Simply turning to the main article would not give you all of the information on Brazil that the encyclopedia holds.

Atlas indexes

A typical index to a book of maps or an atlas will have entries like these:

Acacia Avenue **114** *E8*
Acacia Drive **157** *D8*
Acacia Road **239** *A7*

This example is taken from a street-map atlas. The bold numbers indicate the page in the atlas, while the combination of letters and numbers that follows indicates the square on that page where the streets are found. So Acacia Road is to be found on page 239 in the square labelled A7. These squares are located using 'grid references' in the following way.

FINDING THINGS OUT FROM PAPER SOURCES

There are two sets of grid lines on a map: a set of horizontal lines going from side to side, and a set of vertical lines going down from top to bottom. The lines divide the map up into sections that are each given a particular letter or number. A grid reference marks the point where a particular horizontal section crosses a particular vertical section, so the grid reference 'A7' would mark the point on the map where the horizontal section marked 'A' crosses the vertical section numbered '7'.

	1	2	3	4	5	6	7	8
A							X	
B								
C								
D								
E								
F								
G								
H								

References in indexes

Although it is possible to produce an index using a computer, an experienced human indexer will usually produce something far better. Indexing is a very skilled task. The skill lies in choosing the most appropriate words to describe the information in a section of a book. Indexers have to think which word the reader is most likely to look up to find a particular piece of information, and this may not be the word that is used most in the text.

Good indexes also have *cross-references* which direct the reader to other places which are likely to have information of interest.

A typical index to a book will have entries like this:

Labour movement   see Socialism

This is called a *'see' reference* and indicates that all information on the topic *Labour movement* will be found listed under *Socialism*, elsewhere in the index. There is no information listed under *Labour movement*.

Notice that no page numbers are given in a 'see' reference. It is simply an instruction that if you are interested in the topic *Labour movement* you should look for *Socialism* in the index. Having found that, there will be the standard index entry with page numbers.

There is another type of reference which you will find in an index. This is called a *'see also' reference* and indicates that some information will be found under this term, but related information may also be found under another term.

A typical index to a book might also have entries like this:

*Pets   5, 65, 102–114; see also
Cats, Dogs, Horses, Small
animals*

This time the first index word *Pets* does have page numbers beside it. There is information on *Pets* to be found on page 5, page 65 and pages 102 to 114. However, the indexer has included other areas where there will be information relating to specific pets. Again, no page numbers are given for these references. You are to look through the index to find *Cats, Dogs, Horses* and *Small animals*, and there you will find the pages where there is further information.

> Exercise
>
> Look at the index of your chosen book. Can you identify examples of 'see' references? Can you identify examples of 'see also' references?

Changing the order of words

Most people are familiar with the concept of changing the order of words for a person's name in order to bring the surname to the front.

It can clearly be seen in any telephone directory which is listed alphabetically by surname. If you want to find Sarah Smith's phone number, you need to look for 'Smith, Sarah' in the phone book.

When compiling an alphabetical index, this is sometimes done with words other than personal names.

Example

The following example illustrates a case where this has been done in order to bring together in the list all the entries related to Westminster:

Westbury
Westminster Abbey
Westminster Cathedral
Westminster, University of
Westoverton

There is an entry for the University of Westminster. The indexer has decided that 'Westminster' is the most important word here, bringing it to the front, so that it appears under 'W' rather than 'U'. This means that in this particular index, all the universities with place names in their titles are positioned according to their actual geographical location.

Exercise

Look at the index of your chosen book. Can you identify examples where the word order of a term has been changed?

Information in electronic form

Up until the middle of the 20th century, the main sources for searching for information were all paper-based. Perhaps the best-known example of a paper-based information source is an encyclopedia. Another example would be the current issue of a newspaper.

With the introduction of computers, however, it gradually became possible to transfer the information contained in journals, indexes and encyclopedias onto electronic databases. By the 1970s, computers were widely used to search for information. But this was a complex process, involving the enquirer giving search terms to a librarian or information specialist who would use an electronic terminal to interrogate a database. Some time – possibly several days – later, a print-out of the results of the search would be returned to the enquirer.

Although this may not sound like much of a development from using a paper source, there was a vital difference: it was now possible to move away from only being able to search using one descriptive term or 'keyword' at a time. (We saw in the chapter about finding things out from paper sources that the index of an encyclopedia allows you to look for only one descriptive term at a time.)

Early electronic databases allowed each article of information stored to be described by several keywords. These would be very quickly searched by the computer against the set of input keywords to find the required results. Later, as computer power became even greater and more cheaply available, the searches could be carried out not just looking through the keywords assigned by an information specialist, but generated automatically from the actual text of the information. This is called 'full-text searching'.

So electronic information sources enabled more thorough and faster searching. A key point about electronic data sources in the 1970s and 1980s is that they were subscription services: a library or other organization had to pay an annual fee before it was permitted to search a source. In addition, they were charged for each minute of access of the database, and incurred fairly substantial per-minute telephone connection charges. Because of this expense, searches were only carried out on behalf of senior personnel such as business professionals and university researchers.

Types of electronic information sources

CD-ROMs

With the wider availability of personal computers in the late 1980s, a new possibility arose for storing information electronically. The CD-ROM disk had become a standard removable data-storage medium for use in personal computers. One disk could hold nearly 700 megabytes of information – an enormous amount of data for that period. The capacity of a single CD-ROM was equivalent to the text contained in several years' issues of a newspaper.

So database owners allowed their information to be provided in CD-ROM format. The individual CD-ROM was an expensive item to purchase and they were initially bought mainly by libraries. However, there was now no connection charge and, once purchased, the CD-ROM could be used up to 24 hours per day without incurring any extra cost.

The use of CD-ROMs was not restricted to databases. It was, for instance, possible to put the entire contents of a 30-volume encyclopedia on to one CD-ROM. The cost of the CD-ROM was many times cheaper than the purchase price of the printed encyclopedia. And, of course, you could make a faster and more thorough search using the CD-ROM. CD-ROMs also allowed information to be included in multimedia formats such as audio and video. So instead of reading the text of a famous speech, for example, you could actually hear it for yourself.

The CD-ROM format was also used to produce electronic versions of other types of printed materials, such as atlases, directories and children's books. As disks became more popular, their prices fell to a level where many people could buy them to use on their home computers.

Although CD-ROMs still have a place as sources of information, they have now been largely superseded by the Internet. One reason for this is that a CD-ROM does not contain 'live' data. Once the disk is manufactured, the information on it is fixed and may go out of date.

The Internet

The next big step forward was the wider availability of the Internet during the late 1990s. Although specialized information sources could still command a subscription service, it was in the interest of many other organizations to allow free access as a means of disseminating the information they possessed.

The parallel development of powerful search engines means that the Internet now provides an unimaginably large amount of information on almost any topic you care to choose. Moreover, this is available at little or no cost to the user. The advent of high-speed broadband connections to the Internet means that all sorts of enhanced information in the form of photographs, sound files and video clips is easily accessible.

Groups

In terms of electronic sources of information, a 'group' means any sort of Internet-based system which allows people to discuss topics. Generally a group works by a member sending a question to the group by an e-mail message. This e-mail is forwarded to all members of the group, and other group members will send in their answering e-mails, which are each copied to all group members.

A group is a fairly informal Internet resource and there are groups for discussing hobbies and for social interaction as well as for more serious topics. In many cases it is possible to view the e-mails on the group website without being a member. Joining an appropriate group can be a useful source of information.

Website databases

Many websites offer some sort of searchable database. All sorts of organizations have archives of information that they have built up over the years. Other organizations keep databases of current information. In some cases you are required to pay a fee to search a database, but in a number of cases access or partial access is free.

> **Example**
>
> You can look on the Internet and find electronic versions of almost any newspaper. Most newspapers provide searchable databases of their back issues on their websites. Here are some examples:
>
> http://www.ft.com/home/uk (*Financial Times*)
>
> http://www.guardian.co.uk (*Guardian*)
>
> http://www.independent.co.uk (*Independent*)
>
> http://www.thesun.co.uk (*Sun*)
>
> http://www.timesonline.co.uk (*Times*)
>
> You can search any of these newspapers by typing in your chosen keywords into the search box that appears on the home page – the page that appears when you first go to the site.

Collaborative websites

The services available on the Internet continue to develop. A recent development is the movement away from static websites and web pages towards those which are dynamic. Some of these offer services, such as photo editing and storage, which would have previously only been available by using application software on a computer. Another feature of newer services is that many are designed to allow groups of people to work together and share information.

Some websites encourage visitors to contribute to the site by using a type of software called a 'wiki'. A wiki enables anyone visiting a web page to edit and restructure its contents. This means that the content of the site becomes the product of all of the people who use it, rather than the product of a single person or organization.

Example

A good example of a project that uses this software is Wikipedia, an encyclopedia consisting of 'pages' which the users can update. You can see examples on the Internet at http://en.wikipedia.org/wiki. The idea is simply that people reading this encyclopedia will add further information which they think will be useful. If you look at any article in the Wikipedia, you will see a tab labelled 'edit this page'. If you click on this tab, you can make changes to the article.

Blogs

Another recent development is the 'blog'. The word 'blog' is a shortened form of 'weblog'. This is essentially a diary which is kept on public view via the Web. The owner of the blog can write entries each day, recording what they have done or are thinking about. Obviously many blogs are only of interest to the owner and perhaps the friends of the owner. These are unlikely to be of much help in finding useful information. Moreover, blogs are often short-lived and updated only at the whim of the owner; much of the information found in them is subjective and care must be taken with critical evaluation before using it in an information task.

Nevertheless, blogs can sometimes be sources of valuable and up-to-date information, especially if they are kept by people such as politicians and journalists.

Social networks

There are innovations appearing on the Internet all the time, although not all of these developments are particularly useful for information tasks. One notable phenomenon is the popularity of sites such as *MySpace* and *Friends Reunited* that allow social networking. Typically, these sites provide a place where members can post information about themselves which can be viewed by other members. Although these sites are primarily used for entertainment and social interaction, they can also be sources of information about individuals and about social trends.

Understanding the World Wide Web

What is the Internet?

The Internet is a global network of computers and electronic connections over which information can flow. You can think of this network as being similar to the network of streets in a town. The streets allow all sorts of vehicles to get from one point to another, and there is usually a choice of different routes that can take you from one place to another.

The Internet then is an enormous network which has spread throughout the world. It is capable of transporting not physical goods, as a delivery van would on a road, but all sorts of *information*.

The origins of the Internet go back to the 1960s, when a number of scientific research organizations, each with its own network of computers and terminals, agreed to connect these networks together. No organization assumed overall control, but each organization maintained its own network. Gradually more and more commercial and organization networks were created and joined together.

With time, the Internet extended from research organizations into educational institutions and libraries, and nowadays it has reached the homes of millions of people.

The idea of the Internet can be likened to the road network on the European continent. Each country builds and pays for its own roads but it is possible to drive between any two points on the continent because the road network of each country is connected to that of the next country.

What is the World Wide Web?

You can think of the World Wide Web (also written 'www', and referred to as simply 'the Web') as a collection of data stores from which you can access information. These stores are in fact computers that are connected to one another and to users by the Internet. So the terms 'Internet' and 'World Wide Web' are not identical. The World Wide Web is in fact just one part of the Internet.

As a user of the World Wide Web who wishes to access information, you will normally access it by looking at a website. A website (or just 'site') is a location on the Web. Each website is owned and financed by an organization or person who has the sole right to place information on it.

Governments maintain websites to make information accessible to their citizens. Commercial organizations maintain websites with information about their products to encourage sales. Other information providers similarly create sites to disseminate knowledge. In addition, there are the millions of websites which are paid for and run by individuals who use them to present all sorts of information on subjects such as their hobbies, their favourite music or their family history.

Exercise

Here are the addresses of five websites. Have a look at these different types of website. Can you guess the purpose of each just from the address before you look?

http://www.hmv.co.uk

http://www.ox.ac.uk

http://www.dti.gov.uk

http://www.jobs.nhs.uk

http://www.apple.com/ipod

Who is in charge of the World Wide Web?

No one person or body is responsible for what exists on the Web. (Indeed this is the reason why it can be difficult to enforce laws removing offensive material: there is no overall control and the offending site can be situated anywhere in the world.)

Tim Berners-Lee, the originator of the Web, saw it as a co-operative space for the sharing of information among academic researchers. The Web still can be a research tool, but the main driving force behind its growth has been its use for commercial purposes.

You need to be aware of the very different forces influencing what can be seen on the Web. The information it presents you with is supplied by individuals and organizations who each have their own ideas and agendas. They may often present information in an even-handed way, but occasionally they will mislead you. Unreliable information on the Web ranges from information which is inexact or incomplete, through the repetition of 'urban myths', to information that is deliberately wrong and misleading.

You should therefore think carefully about the information you find via the Internet, making sure that it comes from a reliable source and checking to see that it is correct.

Hyperlinks

A particular attraction in using the Web is the way in which it is possible to move through the pages using 'hyperlinks' (often abbreviated to 'links'). Traditionally these links have been identified on-screen by underlined words. However all sorts of images can be used for this purpose. Sometimes links are shown by words which are not underlined but which change colour when you move the cursor over them with the mouse. The cursor itself usually changes form when passing over a hyperlink.

Here you can see the form of the cursor when it is over non-hyperlink text.

Hodder Arnold FE & Vocational - Market leading resources for students and lecturers.
Hodder Arnold Higher Education & Reference - Innovative textbooks for a range of subjects.
Hodder Arnold Health Sciences - Undergraduate, postgraduate and professional resources in medicine, nursing and allied health.
Hodder Arnold Self-Learning & Improvement - Be inspired - expand your mind and experience in over 750 ways: learn a language, a new skill or hobby.

Here you can see the cursor as an arrow not indicating anything.

Hodder Arnold Self-Learning & Improvement - Be inspired - expand your mind and experience in over 750 ways: learn a language, a new skill or hobby.
Teach Yourself
Michel Thomas - Gain a functional working knowledge of a spoken language in just a few hours.

 Philip Allan Updates

 Chambers **HARRAP'S**
Chambers Harrap
Publishers

Here you can see how the cursor changes when it is over a hyperlink indicated by underlined words.

Hodder Arnold FE & Vocational - Market leading resources for students and lecturers.
Hodder Arnold Higher Education & Reference - Innovative textbooks for a range of subjects.
Hodder Arnold Health Sciences - Undergraduate, postgraduate and professional resources in medicine, nursing and allied health.
Hodder Arnold Self-Learning & Improvement - Be inspired - expand your mind and experience in over 750 ways: learn a language, a new skill or hobby.

Here the cursor is over an image which is a hyperlink.

Harrap's Unabridged Pro CD-Rom

The ultimate French-English English-French dictionary is now available on CD-Rom. Combining the full texts of the Unabridged Dictionary and Harrap's Business Dictionary, the Unabridged Pro is a translator's treasure trove.

Here the cursor is over an image which is not a hyperlink.

Harrap's Unabridged Pro CD-Rom

The ultimate French-English English-French dictionary is now available on CD-Rom. Combining the full texts of the Unabridged Dictionary and Harrap's Business Dictionary, the Unabridged Pro is a translator's treasure trove.

Discount on all book orders

Get 25% off the recommended retail price when you order books online.

Here the cursor is over a non-underlined word which is a hyperlink. Such links may change colour when the cursor passes over them.

Harrap's Unabridged Pro CD-Rom

The ultimate French-English English-French dictionary is now available on CD-Rom. Combining the full texts of the Unabridged Dictionary and Harrap's Business Dictionary, the Unabridged Pro is a translator's treasure trove.

Hyperlinks are used to 'navigate' around a single website and also to move from one website to another (usually a related one). This facility to be able to link from one information source to another is one of the most powerful features of the Internet. Without links it would be very difficult to use the Internet and search for information on it.

The web address system

The World Wide Web holds an unimaginably large amount of information about almost any topic you care to think of. There are billions of pages that can be viewed on it. For the Web to be useful, there has to be a way of selecting the particular page you want to see out of the billions available. To do this you use an application called a 'web browser' or simply a 'browser'. Internet Explorer and Firefox are common examples of browsers.

The pages on the Web are grouped in the form of websites. Each website and each page has its own unique address (called a 'uniform resource locator' or 'URL') which is used to select it for viewing in the browser. On most browsers you can see the URL displayed in a box near the top.

The simplest web addresses are used for home pages. For example, the address of the BBC website's home page is http://www.bbc.co.uk. All the other pages on a website are given addresses based on the home page. So for example, if you click on 'TV' on the BBC's home page, you will go to the first page of the television part of the website. This has the address http://www.bbc.co.uk/tv and you can see that the letters 'tv' have been added to the URL in the browser. If you then go to the BBC1 part of the television section, the URL becomes http://www.bbc.co.uk/bbcone. Usually, the deeper you go into a website, the longer the URL becomes.

Exercise

Go to the government information website at http://
www.direct.gov.uk. (As it opens it will automatically add
the term 'en/index.htm' to the URL.) Try clicking on some
of the links, and note how the URL changes when you
do this. You will see that the longer URLs relate to topics
that are contained deeper in the structure of the website.
For example http://www.direct.gov.uk/en/Employment/
index.htm is the URL if you click on 'Employment'.

Search engines

As the World Wide Web grew in size, it became impossible to
remember all the URLs you might need and so a method had to be
developed to find appropriate websites in another way. The first
technique was to create a list a bit like a telephone directory. The
directory was arranged alphabetically in order of topic. Creating a
directory like this was very time consuming as it had to be done by
people reviewing and categorizing the sites. Even when a relatively
small number of websites existed, the updating of a directory
was a problem because of the time it took to check the websites.
With further growth of the Web it was necessary to speed up the
categorizing of websites by use of an automated system. The result
was the search engine.

What is a search engine?

A search engine is a web-based facility which allows you to find the
URLs of the websites you are interested in. It does this by allowing
you to input keywords that represent your topic of interest and
using these to come up with a list of websites which should be
relevant to your search.

There are many different search engine sites. At the time of writing,
Google is undoubtedly the most popular. Such is its popularity, in
fact, that the verb 'to google' has even entered the English language
meaning 'to search for information on the Internet'. You can use a

search engine to find information on almost any topic. However, the different search engines work in different ways, so you may find that performing the same search using different search engines leads to different results.

Exercise

Search for keyword 'mayflower' on three different search engines. Compare what you find in the layout and types of information displayed. Here are the addresses of three search engines you could try:

http://www.google.co.uk

http://uk.yahoo.com

http://clusty.com

Of course no search engine is perfect and it would be unwise to recommend any one as being better than the rest. It is often a matter of personal preference which search engine is used. For many casual information searches it will make little difference which one you use. However when you are carrying out an important information task, looking for specific and perhaps difficult-to-find information, it is worth trying your search on several search engines to increase the likelihood of a complete and satisfactory answer to your question.

How search engines work

Each search engine is part of a commercial website. Running a successful search engine costs a lot of money and there has to be a means to finance it.

There are two widely used methods for doing this. The first is by selling advertising space on the search engine's web pages. You will notice large 'banner adverts' placed on search engine websites, and there are further adverts for items directly related to your search topic that appear once you have carried out a search. For example, if you type the word 'wine' into the Google search engine, you will get a series of adverts for wine appearing down the right hand side of the results page.

The second model for financing search engines is by charging organizations for 'ranking' – having their website appear towards the top of the list of results produced when a particular keyword is entered into the search engine. At one time this method was frowned upon and seen as a negative feature by those searching for information. Nowadays, however, those using the Internet for shopping see it in a more positive light.

Each search engine uses its own methods to search the Internet, looking at the different websites and their contents. Before a search engine can be used, its developers have done a lot of work already. They have created software which continually scans the Web. This software is often called a 'spider', because it 'crawls' through the Web looking for sites. The spider inspects each website it finds for keywords to categorize it. This results in an enormous database of website addresses and the corresponding words describing them.

When a user comes to enter their chosen search terms, the search engine consults this database and selects the websites that give the best match for them. The methods it uses are extremely complex, giving weight to particular words and taking account of word variations such as plural forms.

Finally, before the search engine lists the sites that match the search, it ranks them in order. You would expect it to put the websites most likely to have the most useful information at the top of the list. However, remember that in some cases commercial enterprises have bought a place near the top of any relevant list of results. The implications of this are that the best sites for your particular search do not necessarily appear at the top of the list. Moreover, the results may appear in a different order if the search is repeated at a later date, as both the contents of the Web and the methods used by search engines evolve.

Metacrawlers

A metacrawler is a special type of search engine. To use a metacrawler you enter search keywords as with any search engine. The difference is that a metacrawler then uses your keywords to search on a number of other search engines. The results it produces are a combination of the results you would get if you carried out a number of searches using each of the search engines in turn.

The advantage of using a metacrawler is that you need only enter the search keywords once to generate a wider spread of results than if only a single search engine were used.

> *Exercise*
>
> Search for keyword 'mayflower' on two different meta-crawlers. Compare what you find in the layout and types of information displayed. Here are the addresses of two search engines you could try:
>
> http://www.dogpile.co.uk
>
> http://www.surfwax.com

The disadvantage of using a metacrawler is that the results will only be as good as the underlying search engines. If these search engines each list a large proportion of commercial enterprise sites in their results, then a combined search may still result in you getting only paid-for advertising sites in your results.

Directories

The web directory was one of the earliest methods for finding information on the Web. A directory is an alphabetically ordered index to the Web, somewhat similar to the subject index in a print encyclopedia. However it is further developed into a 'tree structure', with a number of levels of subcategories. This allows the user to work downwards through the structure, moving at each level to a more specific topic.

Looking at Yahoo directory at http://dir.yahoo.com should help you understand how a directory works. There is a main alphabetical index down the left-hand side of the screen. If you click on a category – for example, 'Entertainment' – a new page will open with alphabetically arranged subcategories such as 'Music' and 'Actors'. This is what is meant by a 'tree structure'. You can then click on these and move even further down the structure. The further down you go, the more precisely you define the search until you end up at the website of an individual entertainer in whom you are interested.

Directories can be very useful in allowing you to home in on sites relating to a specific topic. Early on in the history of the Internet, directories were the only way of searching. As we have seen, however, there are now alternatives.

There are many directory sites to be found on the Internet, but you must be careful. Some of them are poorly maintained, and you should check for signs, such as having up-to-date items listed, that the directory is still 'live', and so likely to be an accurate source of current information.

A definite disadvantage of the directory system is that browsing through the tree structure can be time-consuming and will not automatically lead to a useful result.

Exercise

Go to the Open Directory Project at http://dmoz.org, which is a good example of a well-maintained directory. Start by clicking on 'Regional' and see if you can find websites for buying houses in the English city of Cambridge.

Check your answers on page 132.

Directories and search engines

There can be confusion between directories and search engines because some search engines have directories, while some directories have search boxes. The key difference between the two is that a directory has been compiled by people actually looking at and evaluating the websites listed, whereas search engines use spiders to select websites automatically.

Portals

A portal is another type of Web information-search facility. It is a website which allows you to find information from its many groups of links. You may have met general-purpose portals when you have been 'surfing' the Web. Examples are found on the opening pages of large entertainment and popular information sites.

Many Internet users have a portal site set up as the home page on their computer. This gives them immediate links to lifestyle sites when the browser opens up.

> **Example**
>
> You can see examples of general-purpose portals by looking on the Web at:
>
> http://www.msn.co.uk
>
> http://www.tiscali.co.uk
>
> http://www.aol.co.uk
>
> http://www.orange.co.uk

However, this sort of general portal is not the best to use when looking for very detailed information. There are other portals, which are more specialized in nature, and these can be very useful for information tasks. These are portals set up with the specific aim of providing information. This information could be about medical conditions, hobbies or perhaps environmental concerns.

You can see examples of specialized portals by looking
on the Web at:

http://www.direct.gov.uk/Homepage/fs/en

http://www.health.gov

http://www.trainweb.com

http://www.genhomepage.com

It is worth seeking out specialized portals which cover your own
personal interests and 'bookmarking' them (saving them in your
'Bookmarks' or 'Favourites' file so that you can return to them). They
provide a good starting point when looking for information. You can
search for this type of portal itself by using a search engine. Use the
word 'portal' along with the name of the topic you are interested in
as keywords in your search.

Discussion groups

The term 'discussion group' or simply 'group' covers all the
differently named facilities which allow people to communicate
collectively over the Internet. The various types include:

* groups
* lists
* boards
* forums
* newsgroups
* bulletin boards

There are groups for just about any topic you can think of. Many are
dedicated to scientific and technical subjects. Others have been set
up so that people can discuss their hobbies. A large number are
used merely for social interaction.

Apart from a discussion group's topic of interest, it is important to note whether it has restrictions on membership. Some groups have a closed membership and may be used to circulate semi-confidential information. In these cases only the creator of the group can decide who is invited to join it. However there are many thousands of groups which have open access.

Some groups control what can be posted on them. Groups which are classified as 'moderated', only allow a post to be seen once the person acting as moderator has looked at it to make sure that it is acceptable. A variation on this is where 'reactive moderation' is applied. In this case posts are displayed directly on the group's website but members of the group can alert the moderator to posts they consider unacceptable, and these may then be removed. A great number of groups are not moderated at all.

In the early days of the Web, groups operated by forwarding each post to all the group members by e-mail. Now, however, some merely display the posts on the group website. Group members must visit the site periodically to read the posts.

Often messages that are posted take the form of questions. Other members of the group will then post replies to the original message. This results in a 'discussion' with further postings on the replies.

It is also very easy to set up a group of your own. You can find a number of free group providers on the Web.

Example

Have a look at the web page http://health.groups.yahoo. com/group/diabetes_int/

This is the front page of a group where the topic of common interest is diabetes. If you look down the menu column on the left-hand side, you will see that there is a range of facilities provided. As well as posting messages to the group, the members can place files and photographs on the group website. The group has restricted membership only in the sense that you have to register to view any part of the site. Registering is free and is imposed mainly to control rogue posters. The group is moderated.

Finding things out from groups

Although it may seem a simple enough process to e-mail your question to a group and wait for the answers to come back to you, there are a couple of problems. Firstly you have to locate a suitable group. Of the large number of groups available online, some are of little use for an information task. This may be because the group is poorly used, with only a few posts. Other groups may be ruled out because they receive facetious posts and some groups get swamped with unsolicited 'spam' postings.

Another point is that other group members will expect you to have searched previous group postings to make sure that you are not asking a recently or commonly asked question.

If you are looking for specialized information you will have to take some time to look for a discussion group which focuses on your topic. Going to a website dedicated to the topic may help you find a suitable group. Once you have identified a suitable group, you then need to look through the past postings (which may go back over a number of years) to see if there is one that is related to your own question. Many groups have good search facilities and allow detailed searches to be made. Unfortunately, others offer poor searching.

Example

The website http://www.avforums.com lists a great number of groups covering audio-visual topics. Among these there is a forum dedicated to MP3 players at http://www.avforums.com/forums/forumdisplay.php?f=164. If you look at this forum, you will get a list of the most recent posts. This site also has a good search facility situated near the top right-hand side of the page. You can select 'advanced search', which will allow you to use information such as dates, specific groups and even the name of the person making a post to generate results.

If you cannot find your answer among the past posts, then you can send a new post to ask the question. In almost all cases you will need to join the discussion group before posting. This is usually straightforward. You simply need to supply a valid e-mail address and a nickname for yourself.

The only point to remember is that you are dealing with real people now, not a machine. You need to be polite. It is useful to give a bit of background to your question to help the other group users to answer it as well as they can. You should not use offensive language or post inappropriate images. Of course, if the group is moderated, such posts should be rejected immediately.

Accessing groups through a search engine

Discussion groups started on the Internet early on in its history. These groups (called 'newsgroups') are not related to websites and form a separate part of the Internet called 'Usenet'. They comprise an enormous quantity of information and have been archived. The postings were intended to be accessed by a software application called a 'reader'. This is similar to e-mail in operation and the software is included on most computers connected to the Internet.

There are, however, ways to look at newsgroups and read the postings without using a 'reader'. In particular the Google search engine offers access to newsgroups by searching 'Groups'.

If you go to the Google search engine, you will notice that above the box where you normally type in your search terms there is a row of links beginning: 'Web – Images – Groups – News'.

If you click on the link 'Groups', you will get to Google's newsgroup facility. You can now enter your search terms in the box to search the groups archive. The difference between this and a normal search is that you are now searching Usenet rather than the World Wide Web.

> *Exercise*
>
> Search Usenet for information on housing suitable for keeping rats as pets. (Try using 'cages' and 'rats' as keywords.)

Problems with groups

There can always be problems in searching for information on the World Wide Web, and this is especially true when dealing with groups. The direct human involvement can have certain negative effects:

- Personal opinions may be presented as facts.
- People may mischievously make deliberately misleading posts.
- People may post insulting messages attacking other users – a process known as 'flaming' – especially on sites concerned with controversial topics.

It is therefore particularly important to evaluate any information you find carefully. Furthermore, Usenet groups are often unmoderated. This means that any sort of material can be posted, including untenable points of view and offensive images. So be careful.

Finding things out from electronic sources

You may search for information using a number of different types of electronic source:

* CD-ROMs
* websites
* groups
* searchable databases

However, there are enough fundamental similarities between these types of source to enable the subject of searching them to be treated in a single section.

Basic searching

Most types of electronic information sources require searching using 'keywords'. We have seen that to create keywords, you need to think of just a few words which sum up your search topic. You can then type these into the search box provided by the electronic information source and wait for the resulting answers.

Although the basic search method is common to all types of source, the results that are returned will vary somewhat:

* A CD-ROM of an encyclopedia will give information on your topic in words, visuals or sound format.
* A search engine will give a list of websites which may be of use.
* Groups will generate e-mails from people interested in the topic.
* A website database such as a newspaper archive will give a list of articles related to your search terms.

FINDING THINGS OUT FROM ELECTRONIC SOURCES

Many electronic information sources do not give you a direct answer to your search but instead give you a list of items that may or may not be helpful to you. You need to examine the items in the list and choose which ones you think will lead you to the precise information you are interested in.

Don't worry about capital letters

Almost all electronic searches ignore capital letters. You are probably used to being careful about using capitals correctly when you write, but in electronic searches you don't have to worry about this.

Too much or too little information?

Unless you are very lucky first time, you will find that your search results in either too little information or, just as often, far too much. In both cases this may be due to your choice of keywords. If you find you are given too little information, you must consider using alternative keywords. If it results in too much information, you need some way of cutting it down to a manageable size. Most electronic sources offer an 'advanced search' facility. This gives you ways of restricting the number of results so that you can home in on what you want. For example, you might specify a date range for articles in a newspaper archive so that your search is restricted to articles from a particular day, week, month or year.

It's a machine!

A key point to bear in mind when searching any electronic source is that you are dealing with a machine. Although search engines are becoming more and more sophisticated, the old maxim of 'garbage in – garbage out' still holds true.

You must be very clear in your searching, using as precise terms as possible. Otherwise, you will get results which are not as useful as you would wish.

This applies even to simple matters such as checking that you have keyed in the correct spelling of your search terms and selecting keywords that will find the precise information you are looking for.

It is not an efficient use of your time simply to put in variations of poorly thought-out search terms in the hope that one of them will come up with useful information.

It is also very frustrating to have used a website that provides the answers to your questions and then be unable to find it again. You cannot simply ask the computer, 'Where was that really good website?' So if you find a relevant site, make sure to 'bookmark' it for future reference.

Combining keywords

Typing in keywords which describe your topic will provide you with information that matches keywords. However, when you are looking for very specific information, not only do you need to think carefully about the keywords, you will also need to think how they are best combined.

If you are in the position of asking a knowledgeable person a question, you are able to use complex language to refine your request. For instance, you might say to a travel agent, 'I am looking for information about holidays in the Greek Islands. But I don't want to go to Corfu because I've already been there.'

An electronic source cannot cope with this sort of verbal complexity. There is, however, one method that you can use with an electronic source to make your question more exact. This is called 'Boolean logic' and it has to do with how your chosen keywords are combined. If you do not use this feature, you are leaving the information source to make its own assumptions about how to combine your keywords.

When you input a set of keywords, you can ask yourself the following:

* Are you looking only for results which include **all** the keywords?
* Would results with only **some** of the keywords be useful?
* Would you like to **omit** results that have a particular word?

Boolean operators

There are three Boolean terms which we can use when carrying out an electronic search. We call these Boolean 'operators' because they relate to an operation which is to be carried out. These operators make it clear how the keywords are to be combined.

Let's say you are interested in fishing in the UK. The following might be useful keywords:

- UK
- fishing
- trawlers
- cod
- haddock

The operator 'AND' is used when you want to make sure that the results will have all the keywords present. So if you enter 'uk AND fishing', *all* the results will include both these keywords.

But imagine that you are only interested in fishing for a certain variety of fish.

If we now use 'uk AND fishing AND cod', you will find information about cod fishing in the UK. All the results will include the three words. Because you have made the search more precise, there should be fewer results.

The operator 'OR' is used when looking for results which have *any* of the keywords present. So if you enter 'cod OR haddock', you will find information about cod or haddock. Some results will mention only one of the words, and some will mention both words.

The operator 'NOT' is used when looking for results which specifically do *not* have a particular word present. So if you enter 'fishing NOT trawlers', you will find information about fishing which does not refer to trawlers.

The idea is not too difficult to understand because the three operator names have been chosen so that you can say what is required. Thus AND is used when in ordinary language you would say, 'I am looking for results which have *UK* and *fishing*'; OR is used when in ordinary language you would say, 'I am looking for results which have *cod* or *haddock*'; NOT is used when in ordinary language you would say, 'I am looking for results which have *fishing* but not *trawlers*'.

In fact you can use the AND operator to reduce the number of results you get because it restricts them to having all the keywords present. Conversely, you can use the OR operator to increase the number of results you get because it will include results with any one of the keywords and all the other combinations of the keywords.

Example

If you were searching for information on Internet security, you could use the expression 'internet AND security'. If you then add a further keyword to make the expression 'internet AND security AND banking', you are narrowing down your search. Results which did not include 'banking' will be omitted and you should get results that match your topic more closely.

Exercise

Use Boolean operators to combine keywords to find out about pictures of London around the River Thames.

Check your answers on page 132.

Entering Boolean operators in search engines

The term 'Boolean searching' is used to describe the use of keywords linked by Boolean operators when using electronic information sources.

Unfortunately, different electronic sources implement Boolean searching in different ways. Sometimes, you simply type in AND, OR and NOT. In other systems, special symbols are used to represent the operators, such as + for AND, and – for NOT. So whenever you start using a new electronic source, you should look for instructions which will explain how it allows Boolean operators to be used.

Whatever system a particular search engine uses, almost all have an advanced search facility with entry boxes allowing a type of Boolean operation.

Example

The Google search engine has an advanced search facility that is accessed from its home page by clicking on 'Advanced Search'. If you do this, you will see four boxes for entering your keywords:

- The first box is for 'all of the words'. This means that the results will include all of the keywords you enter here. This is the equivalent of the Boolean operator AND.

- The second box is for 'with the exact phrase'. This means that the results will include the phrase of two or more words you enter here.

- The third box is for 'at least one of the words'. This means that the results will include any one or any mixture of the keywords you enter here. This is the equivalent of the Boolean operator OR.

- The fourth box is for 'without the words'. This means that no results will include the keywords you enter here. This is the equivalent of the Boolean operator NOT.

> *Exercise*
>
> Think about what you would need to enter into the boxes
> on Google's advanced search page to carry out the
> following searches:
>
> 1 Fishing in Fife and Tayside
>
> 2 Fife or Tayside
>
> 3 Tayside, but not Dundee
>
> 4 Fishing in Fife or Tayside
>
> Check your answers on page 132. Now try it out on the
> Internet to see if you get the expected results.

Keeping keywords together

When you carry out a search using a search engine, you can get
disappointing results because the keywords you enter appear in the
text of the results but they do not appear in the same place. This is
particularly the case with very long web pages. In fact it may be not
easy to see where your keywords appear once you open the page.

> **Example**
>
> If you type in an address such as *10 grove place* into a
> search engine you may be lucky and get a fair number of
> correct hits. However, a good number of results will have
> the elements of the address ('10', 'grove' and 'place') in
> separate parts of the page. When we tried it, over 8 mil-
> lion results were returned but not one on the first page of
> results had the keywords together as an address.

The sophistication of search engines is increasing all the time,
but they do not always make very good 'guesses' about word
grouping.

To get round this, you can put your set of keywords within inverted commas. This causes the search engine to treat the keywords as an *exact phrase*. The results will include your set of keywords all together and in the exact order you put them.

Exercise

Try to find out about the indigenous North American group called the carrier people by entering the keywords 'carrier people' into a search engine. What differences do you find when you put in the words with inverted commas and without inverted commas?

Check your answer on page 132.

You may remember that the second of the boxes in the advanced search option of the Google search engine is for 'with the exact phrase'. You can use this instead of inverted commas to keep words together and in the order you wish.

Wildcards

A wildcard is a symbol you use to represent one or more extra letters in a word. In particular you can use it at the end of a keyword to include all the words which use the keyword as its root.

Commonly the question mark symbol (?) is used as a wildcard for one letter, and the star symbol (*) is used as a wildcard for any number of letters (including zero).

Thus entering 'electron*' as a search term will give results including 'electrons', 'electronic' and, of course, the word 'electron' itself. Entering 'electron?', on the other hand, will give results including 'electron' and 'electrons', but not 'electronic'.

In fact, most popular search engines will make their own guesses about whether your search is intended to include plural forms (such as 'electrons') and many do not allow you to enter wildcards. However, you may need to use wildcards when searching encyclopedias on CD-ROMs.

Wildcards can also be used when searching your computer to find a document or file when you are not sure of its exact name.

Dissecting the web address system

A brief explanation of the system used to give addresses (URLs) to web pages was given on page 71.

Most of the time when you are surfing the Web, you can completely ignore the URL of the page you are looking at. However, when you are searching for information and you want to get an idea how reliable it is, then the URL can give some useful clues.

To understand how a URL works, we can look at the BBC's address:

http://www.bbc.co.uk

The letters 'http' stand for 'Hyper Text Transfer Protocol', the code used for all Web pages. This simply means that your browser is looking for a Hyper Text document – a document coded as a web page. The letters 'www' stand for 'World Wide Web'.

The next part of the address is called the 'domain name'. This is the part of the address that differentiates one Web page from another. In this example the domain name is 'bbc.co.uk'.

The final parts of the URL – the parts separated by dots – are called 'extensions'. This example ends in .uk and this indicates that the website has been registered in the United Kingdom. All domain names carry a national identifier as the final extension, except for those registered in the USA.

URL extensions

The information contained in the URL extensions can be demonstrated by looking at the websites of the online bookseller Amazon. There are several websites, each registered in a different country:

- http://www.amazon.com (United States)
- http://www.amazon.co.uk (United Kingdom)
- http://www.amazon.de (Germany)
- http://www.amazon.fr (France)
- http://www.amazon.co.jp (Japan)

If you look at these examples, you will see that some countries, such as Germany, have only a national extension, while some of the others, including the UK, have an extension which seems to give a bit more information about the nature of the website.

UK domain names have an extension '.uk' which shows that they are registered in the United Kingdom and a further extension which shows the nature of the website. Thus for example 'ac.uk' at the end of a URL indicates an academic website, and http://www.manchester.ac.uk is the web address for Manchester University.

Here is a brief list of URL extensions you might encounter in UK addresses:

- ac.uk indicates an academic site
- co.uk indicates a commercial site
- gov.uk indicates a national or local government site
- ltd.uk indicates a registered company
- org.uk indicates an organization, often a charity

A similar system is used in the USA, even though there is no national extension:

- .com indicates any company
- .edu indicates an educational institution
- .gov indicates a government agency
- .mil indicates a military institution
- .net indicates a network provider
- .org indicates an organization (perhaps non-profit)

There are several others (such as .info and .biz) and no doubt new ones will be introduced in the future.

What does the URL tell us?

Discarding the introductory letters 'http://www.', the first part of the domain name may yield useful clues to help you evaluate the usefulness of a website. Is it a well-known name? If your search comes up with a page on the site 'http://www.bbc.co.uk/history' the URL tells you that the page is related to the BBC, a widely respected information provider.

Compare this to an address such as 'http://www.imtotallybonkers. net'. The name of this address might suggest that the person running it does not take life too seriously. It may be an entertaining site to visit, but it is not likely to be a source of reliable information.

What does the URL extension tell us?

Only some of the URL extensions are regulated. The '.gov' and '.ac' are strictly controlled so that they are always assigned to government departments and educational institutions respectively. However, anyone can set up a website with a '.co.uk' or '.org. uk' extension. You cannot assume that the letters '.co.uk' always indicate a commercial company or that '.org.uk' means that the site is necessarily a not-for-profit organization.

The same thing applies to addresses registered in the USA. You can depend on the extensions '.mil', '.gov' and '.edu' meaning what they say, but again anyone can set up a '.com' or '.org' website.

Finally, even the nationality extension may be deceptive. Some countries only allow resident companies to use their nationality extension, but this is not a universal rule. The USA extensions can be used by anyone. The Royal Society of Chemistry uses an American extension in its address (www.rsc.org) even though it is a British institution. So does the British retailer Debenhams (www.debenhams.com).

In summary, you can use the domain name extensions as good clues as to the worth of the information on a website, but be very careful about making definite assumptions. Remember that any individual can set up a website with a convincing domain name to promote their own ideas.

FINDING THINGS OUT FROM ELECTRONIC SOURCES

A warning

Although you might expect that all respected institutions such as universities would be very careful about what is put on their websites, sometimes they give up control over parts of it. This is especially true when students are allowed to have their own websites accessible under the university URL. The longer a URL is, the more likely it is to have only a slight relation to the parent authority. So beware of placing too much trust in pages with this sort of address:

http://www.blankborough.edu/computing/students/
~smithesong/index.htm

Finding things out from people

It is very easy to forget that all information presented in print or electronic form has ultimately originated from a person or a group of people. Sometimes it is possible to bypass a print or electronic source and approach a person directly with a request for information. This is especially valuable when you are looking for information that has not been or may never be published and which is therefore not accessible by other information-searching techniques.

We tend to overlook the fact that people are one of the most valuable sources of information. Yet we all know of people whom we can turn to when we need to know something. For example, when joining a new club, class or workplace you are often told something like 'If you need to know anything, just ask Judy' or 'Tim is the fount of all knowledge around here'. If you are sensible you will make a note of that person's name so that you can go to them later when you need some advice or information.

The best person to ask will vary from one information task to another. If you want to find out about the history of a local graveyard, you might ask a church official, but if you want to find out about horse riding in your area, you might get in touch with the secretary of the local pony club.

Exercise

For each of the following topics, think of a suitable person who could be a useful information source:

1 common ailments of pet dogs

---

2   childhood experiences of those evacuated from London
    during the Second World War

3   objections to new proposals to build a motorway near
    your home

4   leisure activities offered in your area by the local
    council

Check your answers on page 132.

When do people make good information sources?

Although information sources are generally created by people, we rarely consult the creators but tend to use the paper or electronic sources instead. This is because in most cases it is either impossible or inappropriate to communicate with them directly. If they have already provided information in paper or electronic form, they will probably not welcome questions which they feel they have already answered. In some cases you cannot contact the person because they are no longer living.

There are, however, certain situations where it is particularly appropriate to use people as an information sources. They fall into three categories:

* When the person is an **expert** who can quickly supply you with pertinent information from their own knowledge. For example, someone who regularly travels to a European country could tell you about the best ways of flying there.

* When you want to learn about the person's own **experiences**. For example, if you wanted to find out about what it was like to grow up in a farming community in the 1950s, or what life was like in a mining village in Yorkshire during the Miners' Strike of 1984–5, you might interview someone who had lived through that time. Asking people about their experiences is called exploring 'oral history'.

* When you are gathering **opinions** on a topic. In this case, especially with controversial topics, it is important to use a

balanced sample of people and to supplement this with factual information from printed or electronic sources. For example, if you were researching the development of wind farms, the opinions of local people who are for and against a wind farm in an area would add interest to more technical accounts of the environmental and economic benefits and disadvantages of this type of power source.

Exercise

Decide which category these people would fall into if you used them as information sources – a person with expert knowledge, a person with experience, or a person with opinions:

1 a local vet being asked about common ailments of pet dogs

2 an older person being asked about their experience of being evacuated from London during the Second World War

3 the secretary of the local pressure group being asked about her objections to proposals to build a new motorway

4 the manager of a council leisure centre being asked about leisure activities offered by the council

Check your answers on page 133.

You might already know people who could help with your information task. In other cases, you may have to seek out appropriate people.

People who might be useful sources of information include:

* family and friends
* teachers and lecturers
* library or information resource centre staff
* staff of local businesses and organizations
* volunteers in local clubs and societies
* experts in any field of work or leisure

Making contacts

If you need to use a person as a source of information, a most effective way of proceeding is to ask yourself the following three questions:

* **Who should I contact?** You need to contact the people who can provide you with the most useful information. So you have to consider how you will identify the best contacts.
* **How will I contact them?** Will you contact them by letter or e-mail, on the telephone or face to face? Perhaps you will need to use a combination of two or more of these methods of communication.
* **When will I get the information?** You will need to get the information at the appropriate point in your information task. But remember, most people have busy lives and so you must fit in with their schedule.

Who should I contact?

One way of finding useful contacts is simply to ask around. Teachers, lecturers, librarians, business colleagues or other informed sources may be able to point you in the right direction.

You can also use directories, such as a telephone directory, business directories or specialized yearbooks. Two useful sources which you can use to find specialists are *The British Directory of Associations* and *The Charities Digest*, but there are many more. You can also search the Web for useful 'people sources'.

> *Exercise*
>
> Look in your local library or information resource centre and make a note of any directories or other sources which you could use to find contact details of people who are active in your areas of interest and might be useful in an information task.

It is useful to keep a list of potentially useful contacts. For each, you should record their:

* telephone number
* e-mail address
* fax number
* full postal address

It is also useful to get other details such as:

* their position or job title
* their area of expertise
* when in the week they are most likely to be available

It is important that people's contact details are accurate. Wrong information here can delay your progress and be very annoying for all concerned.

How will I contact people?

The answer to this question depends on what sort of information you are looking for. For a straightforward single piece of information a letter or e-mail is best. For more in-depth enquiries you might prefer a telephone or face-to-face discussion. However, if people are located at a considerable distance from you, or your schedules do not permit meeting in person, you may find that you have to gather information for in-depth enquiries through written communication. In this case, you will have to give considerable thought to how to design your request for information – you may need to send a series of questions or a use a short questionnaire.

When will I get the information?

You should try to contact the person as far in advance as possible. Explain why you are asking for their help and indicate what you are looking for and what your deadlines are. Remember that people are busy and will not necessarily see your information task as a high priority. In most cases they are doing you a favour by supplying information or agreeing to be interviewed. So do not presume on their good nature by asking at the last minute.

Preparation

The more preparation you do before contacting the person assisting you in your information task, the more likely you are to get all the information you require. However, the nature of the preparation will vary depending on how you are going about your task.

If you are requesting information by letter or e-mail, it is a good idea to provide a short summary of your information task, showing clearly where the person's input will fit in. If you will be gaining the information over the phone or in a personal interview, make sure that you have thought out all the questions you want to ask. It doesn't make a good impression if you miss out something which you realize is vital to your task and have to get in touch a second time.

If you are in a situation (for example, in a study group) where you know that several other people need to get hold of the same information, it makes sense to get together with them and design a joint request for information or compile a list of questions for use in a group interview.

Recording information

During an interview you will need to make notes of what is said. If the person is willing, you may be able to send a copy of your notes to them once you have written them up. This will give a useful check for accuracy on the information you have gained. If you are gathering people's experiences and opinions, it might be helpful to ask if you can make an audio recording of the conversation. This will allow you to make an accurate transcription into written form later. With the interviewee's permission, you can take photos of people and places with a digital camera or your mobile phone. If the person lends you something such as a photograph or a letter, make sure that you treat it with care and return it as soon as you have finished with it.

And finally

Most important of all, remember that the person providing you with information is doing you a favour. So don't forget to write or e-mail to thank them afterwards. If you are getting information for a written project, the people you used as sources should also be acknowledged in your finished work.

Dealing with information

In the preceding chapters we have looked at where you can go to find information and how you can go about looking for information in these places. This chapter considers how you can use information effectively once you have found it. It deals with three separate topics: evaluating information, intellectual property, and references.

Evaluating information

When you carry out a detailed information task, you will spend a lot of time deciding exactly what you are looking for and then carry out searches. But even when you have found items of information you are not yet finished. You still need to evaluate the information you have found. This means making sure that you have found exactly what you set out to look for. To do this you need to ask three questions:

- Is the information suitable?
- Is the information current enough?
- Is the information reliable?

Is the information suitable?

It may seem obvious that you would never knowingly choose to use information that was not suitable for your information task. However, you really do need to check each piece of information to be sure that it is appropriate.

Imagine that you are trying to find out about the oil industry to write a report. The Internet has enormous amounts of information on this topic and it is easy to find articles by performing a search using the keywords 'oil industry'.

The following websites might be returned from such a search:

http://www.coconutoil.com/John%20Kabara.pdf

http://tonto.eia.doe.gov/oog/info/gdu/gasdiesel.asp

http://news.bbc.co.uk/1/hi/programmes/
newsnight/4354269.stm

http://dictionary.kids.net.au/word/oil_industry

If you look at these sites, you will find that the first one is a presentation on the uses of coconut oil, the second shows the price variations in motor fuel prices in the USA, the third is an article from 2005 about plans for the use of oil in Iraq and the fourth is a definition of the term 'oil industry' for children. If you consider the different natures of these articles, it becomes clear that there is a huge variation in the amount of detail given and in the type of language used. Clearly one of the articles is far too simple for a report aimed at an adult readership.

It is all too easy to use the Internet to find articles related to your topic area that are not suitable for your purposes!

Setting criteria for suitability

In order to evaluate the information you find, you need to check it against a set of *criteria*. To do this, you should go back and remind yourself of the question you set out to answer and produce a set of standards which you can use to judge the information.

You can set up the criteria near the start of your task, before you actually find any information. Doing this enables you to evaluate information as soon as you find it.

In deciding on criteria for suitability, there are three points to consider:

* There should be a close match between the information and the topic area of the information task. At first glance this seems so obvious as to be not worth stating. However, it is important to look closely at the information to see that it matches your needs. Simply looking at the title is often not enough: a title

may be misleading because it uses ambiguous words, or it may even be deliberately misleading (perhaps a joke or a hoax).

- You must establish what depth of information you need. The range of information offered by different sources may vary from shallow overviews of a topic to very detailed descriptions which may be many pages long.

- You must establish the most desirable level of language to match your understanding. If you are looking for information in an area that you know little about, you will need to find information presented in simple everyday terms. On the other hand, it may be that you already have some knowledge of the subject. In this case you may set your criteria for language level rather higher. Some information may be available in a foreign language; if you cannot read this language, this information is of no use to you.

Investigating suitability

Once you have established your criteria for suitability, you can evaluate information simply by reading it.

However, a useful preliminary check is to consider the *purpose* of the information source. Ask yourself what the person providing the information is aiming to achieve. It may be:

- to educate
- to entertain
- to inform
- to persuade
- to promote
- to sell

Thinking about this should help you to decide whether the source is a suitable one for you to use and it will also inform your thinking as you go through the criteria for suitability that you have established.

The depth of coverage and the level of language used in a piece of information are very much related to its intended audience. So consider the intended audience for the information. This may be:

- business people
- college students
- members of the general public
- interested amateurs
- professional people
- researchers
- school pupils
- experts
- university students

If you can see that the information has the purpose of entertainment and the intended audience is college students, then you probably cannot depend on the information being particularly useful when looking for detailed technical data.

Similarly if the purpose is to advertise and sell a product to the general public, then it is probable that the information does not have much depth and the language level is fairly low. Such information will certainly not reveal any shortcomings in the product being sold.

Exercise

Look at the following examples from the Web and decide what the purpose of the information contained is and for what audience it is intended.

http://phys.educ.ksu.edu

http://yahooligans.yahoo.com/content/jokes/
category?c=37

Is the information current enough?

When you find a potentially useful source of information it is often important to know when it was published. For instance, if you were interested in the population statistics for a country and used an encyclopedia published ten years ago, or a website which has not been updated since the year 2000, you will get an answer that may be significantly different from the current population.

The rate at which information becomes out of date in technological subjects is even more dramatic. For example, the speed at which personal computers work has increased enormously due to technological advances, and an article written ten years ago will give values for typical personal computer systems which are very different from the present-day values.

For other types of information task, however, the currency of the source is not critical. Verifiable historical facts do not vary with time. If you are trying to find the date of Britain's entry into the Second World War, it does not matter if you consult a reference book published in 1980 or 2004. Both will give the same answer.

Setting criteria for currency

If you are looking for information which does not change with time, then the key date to establish is the date when the information first appeared. So if your information task is to find out details of the structure of London's Tower Bridge, you can find out when it was built. Clearly information sources published before this date will not contain the relevant information. Sources published after this date would be more suitable. So the currency criterion is for information published from say, 1890 to the present date.

If the task concerns information which changes with time, then you have to decide the time point you are interested in. For example, if you were going on holiday and needed to find the exchange rate for buying euros, you would need today's rate. The rate one year ago would not be of any use to you.

On the other hand, if you are exploring public opinion about the relationship between Spain and England during the period of the Spanish Civil War, then your currency criterion would be for information originating in the period under investigation – that is, 1936 to 1939.

Decide which of the following require you to check the currency of the information found:

1 the cost of a driving test

2 the middle name of Margaret Thatcher

3 the distance between Cardiff and Newcastle

4 the name of the French Prime Minister

5 the main industries employing people in Doncaster

Check your answers on page 133.

Investigating currency

To evaluate the currency of information you need to find a date which is associated with it. Sometimes this may be easy to find, but even if it is difficult you still need to try to find it. The methods you might use will depend on the type of source you are dealing with.

Currency of paper sources

Most paper sources actually have a date printed on them:

- Books have the date of publication on the back of the title page.
- Atlases are really books of maps and similarly have the date of publication on the back of the title page.
- Maps should have the date on the title or key area, sometimes at the lower right-hand side of the map itself.
- Leaflets often have the date printed on the outside at the end of the last page.

Many reference books were first published some years ago and new updated versions come out every so often. Typical publication information for a reference book will read something like this:

First published 1987
Revised 1995

Revised 2005
Reprinted 2006

This tells you that although the book was printed in 2006, the information cannot be more recent than 2005 when it was last revised. The information may in fact have been recorded as long ago as 1987.

Exercise

Choose a reference book, such as a dictionary, and open it and look for its date of publication. You should see it on the reverse of the title page.

Currency of people sources

When dealing with people as an information source you can only rely on asking them about the currency of what they are describing. You can use questions such as these to get a useful estimate of the date of their information:

* When did you find out about this?
* Is this the latest information you have about the topic?
* When was the last time you tried this yourself?

One problem in using a people source is that a person's memory can sometimes be unreliable. It is useful if you can get some sort of additional confirmation of the date. You might try to get the person to tie in the date of the information to being around the same time as a verifiable historical event. For example, if they say, 'I am sure it was around the time of the start of the Millennium celebrations, because we passed the Dome on the way', you can be fairly confident about the date.

Currency of electronic sources

Some electronic sources such as CD-ROM encyclopedias display their date in the same way as books. You will find the date of publication on the packaging of the CD-ROM or printed on the disk itself.

When dealing with information found on Internet groups, you can look at the dates of the postings. This lets you know when the information was put up on the group. Remember, however, that you are again dealing with a people source here. You may be able to post to the group or e-mail the person who made the original post to ask questions to help verify the date. Another method would be to look for clues appearing in other related postings (such as replies to the original post) that confirm the currency or date of the information.

A real problem exists however with dating the information found on Internet websites. There is no recognized or compulsory method used and many websites have little indication of their currency.

You can get an idea on some websites as to how recent the information is because there is a 'last updated' date clearly shown on the website (often at the end of the home page). This is a very useful feature but it is not provided on all websites. Also this date could refer to an updating of only one section and not the one you are interested in.

If the website you are looking at has no 'last updated' feature, then the next step is to look for dates elsewhere on the site. There may be a section on the website called 'What's New' or 'What's On'. The latest dates mentioned in such a section will indicate whether the site appears to be well maintained and kept up to date.

If there are no dates to be found anywhere on the website, then the only way you can hope to get an idea of currency is to draw conclusions from other things. For instance, for a website which describes a famous person who died in 2005 as being alive, it is clear that the information is not current.

Exercise

Look at the following websites and assess their currency:

http://www.factmonster.com/ipka/A0004379.html

http://www.welshcycling.co.uk

http://www.qca.org.uk

http://www.treesforlife.org.uk

http://www.mascot.uk.com

Is the information reliable?

It is also important to consider whether the person or organization that produced the information is likely to be truthful and impartial.

Let's go back to our example of trying to find out about the oil industry to write a report. If you enter your keywords into a search engine, you will be directed to websites maintained by a variety of people and organizations. These may include personal blogs, sites maintained by environmental pressure groups and sites of oil companies.

There is unreliable information to be found in all types of source – paper sources, people and electronic sources. The Internet has something of a reputation as a haven of hoaxes and misinformation, but books and other paper sources can also contain unreliable information. People may make mistakes due to faulty understanding or poor memory. In other cases, sources deliberately present information in a biased way in order to create a false impression of the strength of an argument.

Setting criteria for reliability

Once again, you need to set criteria to make sure that you can trust the information you have found:

* Information must be **accurate**. Dates and numbers as well as statements of facts should be correct.
* Information should have **authority**. It should ideally have been produced by a person or organization which has built up a reputation for being trustworthy over a period of time.
* Information should **lack bias**. It should not suppress certain facts and emphasize others in order to give a false impression of the truth.
* Information must be **authentic**. It should have been produced or provided by the stated author using the methods claimed.

For the majority of information tasks, the reliability of the information is paramount.

Investigating accuracy

It is important that you are confident that your findings are accurate. The only method for evaluating the accuracy of information, without personal specialized knowledge, is that of comparing it against other sources. In some cases you can do this fairly easily.

> **Example**
>
> You have found a figure for the population in the year 2001 for the United Kingdom of 58,886,000.
>
> You could check this figure using data from other sources which carry this type of information:
>
> • National Statistics, the government statistics service
>
> • The World Book Encyclopedia
>
> • Wikipedia (http://en.wikipedia.org)

However for some tasks it may not be so easy to find alternative sources with which to compare. In such cases you may have to make a judgement about reliability based on the authority of the source.

Investigating authority

In many situations, you can be sure of the information when you can trust the source of the information. If the writer or the publisher of the information has *authority*, this means that they have built up a reputation for providing good and accurate information over a period of time.

To establish the authority of the information you need to:

• Find the identity of the author and publisher of the information. The author may be an organization, a group of people or a single person.

• Establish that the author or publisher of the information is expert in the field. It may be that the author is unknown but that the publisher is renowned for good quality products providing reliable information.

> *Exercise*
>
> Look at this website http://www.healthyliving.gov.uk, which covers the topic of health guidance. Decide who is responsible for it and whether you would trust this source.
>
> Check your answer on page 133.

Primary and secondary sources

We can divide information sources into primary and secondary sources. A primary source is one that contains original information, for example a research paper on experiments on a new flu vaccine. A secondary source is a second-hand account, which may be affected by the way the information has been interpreted, for example a newspaper article which simplifies the flu-vaccine research so that it can be understood by a general readership. You may feel that you can rely more on a primary source of information rather than a secondary one, but this is not a hard and fast rule.

Although a primary source will present original information, it does not always mean that this information is reliable. An original document may still contain incorrect or biased information.

> *Exercise*
>
> For each of the following information sources, decide whether they are primary or secondary:
>
> 1 archived committee minutes
>
> 2 autobiographies
>
> 3 biographies
>
> 4 encyclopedias
>
> 5 government statistics

6 literature reviews

7 newspaper advertisements

8 newspaper feature articles

9 newspaper reports written during an event

10 popular magazine articles

11 speeches

Check your answers on page 133.

Checking for bias

Bias is the presentation of information from only one point of view, so that alternative viewpoints are excluded. When information is supplied by one person, it may be that they emphasize a particular viewpoint unconsciously because of their cultural background or their personal opinions. Biased information from an organization, however, is more likely to be the result of the organization's desire to promote a particular viewpoint or to suppress information about something.

Of course for some information there may only be one point of view. A good example of this is a scientific rule: there is no scope for bias in the statement that there are 1,000 metres in a kilometre.

But bias is possible in all sorts of areas. Information can be affected by cultural, ideological, political or religious viewpoints. It may be possible to detect bias simply from the way in which the information is presented. If not, it may be possible to find out whether there is any aspect of the author or publisher's background that might cause you to suspect them of bias.

Another cause of bias is commercial interest. This may involve something as simple as a company promoting information which just happens to recommend goods and services that it produces itself. In more serious cases, the company may be suppressing information which reveals unfavourable facts about its products or activities.

If you do find bias in the information you have found, you do not necessarily have to discard the information. It may be that the area you are searching is a controversial one in which all of the sources push their own particular viewpoint. In this case you can use the information, but you should also look for information given from other points of view.

The Web is an important information source, so most organizations pushing particular points of view and wishing to influence people have websites outlining their opinions.

Example

Here are some websites maintained by pressure groups. You would expect them to present information that gives priority to a particular point of view:

http://www.ash.org.uk

http://www.foe.co.uk

http://www.sone.org.uk

When dealing with controversial topics it is important to seek out information giving a complete view of the area. You need to seek out and compare information supplied by the various and sometimes opposing groups.

Exercise

Look for information about congestion charging for private cars on the websites of different political parties, such as these:

http://www.conservatives.com

http://www.labour.org.uk/home

http://www.libdems.org.uk

See if you can detect bias in the way the different parties present information about the issue.

Investigating authenticity

Finally, in looking at the subject of reliability, there is the question of authenticity. It is important that you know that the sources of your information are authentic – that the author and publisher are in fact who they say they are.

With paper sources, the most likely (although rare) difficulty is that the information is in fact part of a hoax or joke. One example is a range of humorous guide books written about imaginary holiday destinations.

It is easy and inexpensive to set up a website. There are many websites which can be deceptive: they look like the real thing but are not. Some are simply done as a joke, but others are more serious.

> Exercise
>
> Look on the Internet at these four websites and judge the authenticity of each:
>
> http://www.skyhighairlines.com/main.asp
>
> http://home.inreach.com/kumbach/velcro.html
>
> http://www.whitehouse.org
>
> http://www.easyclimatechange.com

All you can do is to be aware of the dangers and always try to double-check your information against alternative sources.

Intellectual property

The subjects of intellectual property rights and copyright can be complex and can give rise to prolonged legal disputes. You should be aware of both concepts when you carry out an information task so that you can avoid being accused of breaking the law. Due to the complexity of these subjects, only a general overview can be given here. If you are in any doubt about the legality of your actions, you should check the situation with someone with expert knowledge.

Intellectual property rights

'Intellectual property' is the term used to describe things that a person has spent time thinking about and creating. These are not necessarily physical things you can touch. Examples of intellectual property would be:

* a method of making computer chips
* a novel
* a song recorded on a CD
* a new design for a wallpaper pattern
* the logo used to identify a particular brand of sportswear

These are just some types of intellectual property. In each case, we are dealing with the product of a creative thought process.

Intellectual property rights allow creators to have ownership over their creations. These rights mean that the creator can:

* make money by selling the use of the creation
* control how it is used

As an example, if you invented a new machine which converted waste plastics into useful building material, you could patent it. Having a patent makes it clear that you are the inventor and holder of the intellectual property rights and means that other people cannot use the invention without your agreement. You would normally give your agreement only if you were paid an appropriate amount of money. So you have the right to decide if, where, when and by whom your invention may be used and you are then rewarded for your creativity.

The process of obtaining a patent for an invention involves registering it with a national patent office. This allows it to be seen by other people but prohibits them from simply copying it. Anyone wanting to exploit the invention would have to come to a financial agreement with the person awarded the patent. A patent lasts for a fixed period of time, after which the invention can be exploited by anyone without restriction. Currently, in the United Kingdom, once a patent is granted, it must be renewed every year after the fifth year, giving a maximum of 20 years' protection.

Copyright

Copyright is the name given to the laws which apply to the intellectual property rights of literary and artistic material. These copyright laws exist to prevent unauthorized copying of materials. They cover a large range of materials such as fiction and non-fiction books, music, audio recordings, films, software and broadcasting. The protection given to a creator by copyright is automatic in the United Kingdom. The creator does not need to register that they have written a new song or made a recording. There is no equivalent or need for a patent for literary and artistic materials.

There is a set of rules determining how long copyright lasts for each of the different classes of material. Currently, in the United Kingdom, for a book or a magazine article, the copyright lasts until 70 years after the death of the author. On the other hand, the copyright for a music recording lasts only 50 years after its publication.

Although there are many legal complexities surrounding the concept of copyright, as with all intellectual property rights, its main purpose is to allow people who create things both financial reward and control over how their creation is used.

This means that when you are carrying out an information task, you must be aware of the limits that copyright places on you.

Copyright infringement

The term 'copyright infringement' refers to breaking the law of copyright. There are many ways of doing this, intentionally or otherwise.

Exercise

Which of the following would be a copyright infringement:

1 Borrowing a novel and copying it page for page on a photocopier, so that you have a copy of your own.

2 Using a computer scanner to make your own copies of part of an Ordnance Survey map.

---

3 Making copies of a software package and giving them to your friends to save them money.

4 Burning a CD copy for yourself from a music CD which your sister has purchased.

5 Downloading a photograph of your favourite band from their website and printing colour copies of it for your friends.

6 Selling DVDs of popular films you have copied at home.

7 Making ten photocopies of one poem from a book of newly published poems.

Check your answers on page 134.

The strict nature of copyright law means that you cannot, for example, photocopy large sections of books and include them in a project or make multiple copies of even a small portion of a book.

Strictly speaking, without the permission of the creator of the work, you cannot make a copy of any part of any work, whether in the written, audio or video medium. However, there are some accepted practices which you can make use of:

- It is not illegal to create a copy of a literary work by writing it out by hand.
- Partial waiving of copyright is given for study purposes.

Fair dealing in education

The concept of fair dealing for non-commercial research or study is part of the UK copyright legislation. It means that when you are studying, you may make a *single* copy of a part of a literary work for study purposes. Note that this does not apply to media such as films or audio recordings.

Unfortunately, the legislation does not give an exact definition of how big a part of a book you can copy. However, it is generally accepted that copying up to 5 per cent of a book and no more than a single chapter will not be seen as a copyright infringement. Similarly you should be safe to copy one article from a magazine or newspaper – provided, of course, that it is to be used solely for study purposes.

You will usually find that schools, colleges, universities and public libraries are very strict about this. Notices are usually placed near photocopiers in libraries with warnings about infringing copyright. Although a library is not legally responsible for an infringement – the person who makes the copy certainly is – there is a duty to make sure that law-breaking does not occur on its premises. If you are in any doubt about this, then ask the advice of the library staff.

Copyright and the Internet

It is generally the case that what is illegal in the 'real world' is also illegal on the Internet. This means that all the contents of websites on the Internet are covered by copyright law, just as if they were books on a library shelf.

If you are working on a computer at home, with no librarian keeping a watch on you, it is very easy to copy all sorts of things from the Web and you do not even need to pay for photocopying. But remember: this is still breaking the law!

Plagiarism

'Plagiarism' is the term for copying someone else's work and claiming it as your own. You can fall into the trap of plagiarism if you copy, say, a paragraph from a book by putting it into a report and not clearly stating that it is someone else's work. This is really a separate issue from copyright and has nothing to do with photocopying. If you copy the paragraph in your own handwriting into your report and do not acknowledge the person who wrote the original or provide a reference to the book you found it in, then you have still committed plagiarism.

It can be quite easy to do this. You may simply forget to put in the source of the material in your own work, or you might include the material because you think it is better than what you could do.

These are not excuses, however!

Do not try to get round this issue by copying a whole paragraph and then changing a couple of words. Plagiarism will still be obvious. Remember that quoting from respected authorities adds weight to your report, rather than detracting from it. But you must always give references to any material you have not written yourself that is included in a report. (The subject of how to create references is covered on pages 122–3.)

One of the dangers of using the Internet is that it makes it very easy to plagiarize. You can use the 'copy and paste' function to extract large portions of text without the effort of copying from a book. Educational authorities in particular are quite aware of this and use sophisticated software to detect plagiarism in coursework submitted by students.

References

The end-product of your information task might be an essay, a project report or a presentation. In each case it is important to provide details of the information sources which you have used in order to produce your work. This is called 'referencing'.

Why are references necessary?
You reference the sources you have used for three reasons:
* People who read your work may want to find out more by following up some of the sources you have consulted. Providing details of each source makes this easier for them.
* By showing that you have consulted reliable and authoritative sources, you add weight to your own work.
* You avoid any accusations of plagiarism – taking someone else's work and attempting to pass it off as your own.

There are many accepted systems for creating and arranging references in your work, but there is only space to illustrate one commonly accepted system here. If your information task is related to school, college or university coursework, it is a good idea to check with your tutor and find out if they wish the references to be done in a different way from the system which follows.

What should be referenced?

In your information search you will undoubtedly have consulted information sources which looked promising initially but in the end did not yield any relevant information. There is no need to reference these. In fact, it would be unhelpful to yourself or your readers to do so.

You should, however, reference any source which provided you with:

- useful background information
- specific theories or ideas which you have included in your work
- facts, such as historical, geographical and scientific information or statistics
- actual quotations taken directly from people, paper or electronic sources

Showing the references

References for specific quoted information have to be indicated in the text of your report in some way. This is most easily done by using successive numbers.

Here is an example of text from a report that includes references:

The findings of the Baker Group[17] have shown that there is a great need for increased mobility. On the other hand the paper by Professor Martin[18] has shown the disadvantages of increased mobility on the ecosystem.

There are two references and they are indicated as '[17]' and '[18]'. You can use one set of consecutive numbers to number all of the references in the whole report.

Having added numbers to the references in the text, you now have to decide where to record them in your project. They are commonly included in one of two ways: either added at the foot of each page as they occur in the text, or collected and placed at the end of your report in a 'list of references'.

An alternative method of referencing sources is to list the source material at the end of your text in alphabetical order by author surname. In this case there is no need for numbers, but the surname of the author, the date of publication and (if available or relevant) the page number of the source material are given within the text, as in the example below:

A recent study (Davies, 2007) highlights the growth in demand for local produce, although Smith and Jones (2006) conclude that almost half the adult population is oblivious to the origin of the food they buy.

How to reference paper sources

If you look at reports written by other people, you will see examples of how to reference sources. There are many systems of referencing – the important point is that you adopt one system and use it consistently. Here are some examples of how to reference straightforward sources using one widely used system.

Books

The general format is:

Author surname, Author forename (year published). *Book title.* Place published, name of publisher.

For example:

Smith, Melanie (2006). *Fashion stereotyping in teenage girls.* London, Fonda Press.

Newspaper or journal articles

The general format is:

Author surname, Author forename (year published). 'Article title'. *Magazine title*, **volume number**, page numbers of article.

For example:

McArthur, Michael (2005). 'The croft clearances in Caithness.' *Scottish Historical Times*, **22**, 55–62.

How to reference electronic sources

CD-ROMs

The general format is:

Author surname, Author forename (year published). *CD-ROM title.* Place published, name of publisher. [CD-ROM].

For example:

O'Riley, James (2004). *Animals of the Northern hemisphere.* Glasgow, Tinkerbell Publications. [CD-ROM].

Note that the last item in square brackets indicates the format of the source. You can adapt this for other non-print formats by adding other descriptions, for example '[DVD]'.

Websites

Because websites are constantly changing you must give not only the details of the website but also indicate the date on which you accessed the information. The preferred format for the date is with the month in words:

2 April 2007

If you can find the author and web publisher details, website references can look similar to those for a book. For example:

Robertson, Meg (2006). *Referencing explained.* [online]. Melford, Dundrum College.
Available at: http://www.dundrum.ac.uk/libinf/documents3
[Accessed 5 October 2006]

If there is no author or publisher, simply give the details you can gain from the home page. For example:

Mascot Modern apprenticeship summary database.
Available at: http://www.mascot.uk.com
[Accessed 5 October 2006]

| Exercise |

Find these reports:

http://www.law-lib.utoronto.ca/investing/reports/rp1.pdf

http://www.law-lib.utoronto.ca/investing/reports/rp30.pdf

http://www.infed.org/archives/e-texts/individualization_and_youth_work.htm

Look at how the references are laid out and how the bibliographies are ordered. Do you find the systems adopted clear and easy to use?

(You will find that the way the references are laid out or arranged differs from the approaches which are outlined above. However, you should find that each bibliography is consistent within itself.)

A final tip

Do note down or bookmark the details for any information source you have used *at the time you are using it*. It can be extremely frustrating and time wasting to have to retrace your steps to retrieve this bibliographical information at a later date.

Reviewing the process

When you look back on any task which has been undertaken, you will usually see some things which, if the activity were to be repeated, would be better approached in a different way. As the saying goes, 'Hindsight is a wonderful thing.'

You are unlikely to repeat the same information task twice. However, it is likely that you can learn general lessons from one information task and apply these to future tasks. If you are required to carry out an information task as part of coursework at school or college, you may even be required to carry out a review of your activity as part of the assessment. In any case, it is worth reviewing your information-searching experience, identifying what worked well and what didn't work so well, and then using these lessons in the future.

We have already seen that it is necessary to evaluate the information which you have found in order to demonstrate that it is suitable for your purposes. What we are looking at in this section is different. We are not reviewing the actual information but reviewing the *process* by which it was found.

To review the information searching process, it is useful to look at:

- the **choice of keywords** and the method by which they were chosen
- the **choice of information sources**
- the **search strategy**

As you read through this section, it will be useful to keep in mind an information task which you have recently undertaken.

You probably did some fine-tuning of your information-searching process as you went along. As you look at the questions which follow, think back to any changes you made to your original plan and consider why you changed your approach at these points.

Choice of keywords

In reviewing your choice of keywords, you need to think about following questions:

* How did you choose the keywords initially?
* Was this the best way of making the keyword choice?
* Did you have to change the keywords as your information search progressed?
* If changes were made, what were the reasons for these?

> **Think for a moment** about how this worked for your own information task. Note down your ideas.

These are some of the problems you might have had with your in choice of keywords:

* They were too specific, resulting in not enough information.
* They were too broad, resulting in too much information.
* They were inaccurate, producing information which was not relevant to your topic.
* They were too technical, leading to information which you di not understand.

Choice of sources

In reviewing your choice of information sources, you need to th about the following questions:

* How did you choose your information sources initially?
* Was this the best way of making the choice?
* If you were undertaking this information task again, are there any sources which you consulted that you would not use again? If so, what was the reason for this?

> **Think for a moment** about how this worked for your own information task. Note down your ideas.

These are some of the problems you might have had with your initial choice of information sources:

- They were difficult or time-consuming to use.
- They were inconvenient to access – perhaps you had to travel some distance to use them and the time and effort spent was not matched by the usefulness of the information you found.
- They did not yield the information which you expected.
- They produced information which was too simple, too complex, biased, out of date, insufficient, or in an inappropriate format.

Search strategy

In reviewing your search strategy, you need to think about the following questions:

- Before you started your information search, you decided on an order in which to work through your chosen sources. Did you find that this order worked well or did you have to change it?
- If changes were made, what were the reasons for these?
- Did one source lead logically on to another?
- Did you find you happened by accident upon relevant sources that were not in your original search strategy and ended up using these?
- How could you have devised a search strategy which would have included these additional sources?

> **Think for a moment** about how this worked for your own information task. Note down your ideas.

These are some of the problems you might have had with your initial search strategy:

- It produced information in an illogical order – perhaps you came across very detailed data before general background information.

- It did not fit in with your timescale for the information task
  – perhaps one of the people sources may only have been
  available for you to interview on one specific day.
- It led you up dead ends or round in circles.
- It concentrated too heavily on one type of information source
  – perhaps on electronic sources at the expense of people and
  paper sources.

Summary

Now you have considered your overall approach to your information
task and answered all of the questions about your choice of
keywords, your choice of sources and the way you designed your
search strategy. You should be able to summarize your thinking
using these three headings:

- What worked well in my information task?
- What did not work as well as expected in my information task?
- What would I do differently (and why?) with a similar
  information task in future?

Thinking about these things will help you to be more efficient in the
future when you set about the task of finding things out.

In search of information

Exercise on page 3

1 This is an information task where you are likely to want a great deal of information. Buying a house is a major financial transaction and you would want to research different areas of the city and their facilities, such as transport links, types of houses available, typical selling prices over the last few months, and any planned developments such as a new shopping mall. You might also want to research estate agents, their prices and services in order to choose one.

2 This is a fairly straightforward task, assuming you are not a doctor investigating obscure symptoms of the disease.

3 This is straightforward. The answer will be short and simple.

Exercise on page 4

1 This is a straightforward task, requiring information at a simple level.

2 This technical task will result in information at a complex level, using specialized language.

3 This is a medium-level task. Although the procedures may have some complexity, you will want the information in layman's terms.

ANSWERS TO EXERCISES

Exercise on page 10

1 symptoms, measles

2 colour, cornflower (The noun 'flower' on its own is not enough to really describe this topic. It is too general.)

3 director-general, who (The organization is usually referred to by its abbreviated title. However, if you did not find information using this as a keyword, you could search using the full name.)

Exercise on page 11

1 joiner, woodworker

2 error, blunder

3 verse, rhyme

Exercise on page 12

1 one complete rotation *or* a bicycle

2 sewing thread *or* a tall story

3 children *or* young goats

Information on paper

Exercise on page 21

1 Books

2 Periodicals

3 Posters

4 Pamphlets

5 Manuscripts

Exercise on page 24

1 Fiction

2 Fiction

3 Non-Fiction

4 Fiction

5 Non-Fiction

6 Non-Fiction

ANSWERS TO EXERCISES

Exercise on page 27
1 Glossary
2 Title page
3 Preface

Exercise on page 36
1

2

3 Castle

4

Exercise on page 44
Tabloid: *The Sun*, *The Daily Express*, *The Daily Mail*, *The Daily Mirror*
Broadsheet: *The Independent*, *The Guardian*, *The Daily Telegraph*

Finding things out from paper sources

Exercise on page 50
1 Craft, cruiser, dinghy, ferry, ship, vessel, yacht
2 You could find the sections on *shipping*, *delivery* or *transport*.

Exercise on page 54
1 East Anglia
  East Longtown
  Eastabington
  Eastleigh
  Easton

2 Eastabington
  East Anglia
  Eastleigh
  East Longtown
  Easton

Exercise on page 54
Ashton Railway
Ashton Rd
Ashton Rowing Club
Ashton Secondary School
Ashton Stonemasons
Ashton St

ANSWERS TO EXERCISES

Exercise on page 55

7 o'clock

7 Up

76 Arran Road

Seven Brides for Seven Brothers

Seven times seven

Seventy-six Trombones

Seven Brides for Seven Brothers

7 o'clock

Seven times seven

7 Up

76 Arran Road

Seventy-six Trombones

Information in electronic form

Exercise on page 76

Regional – Europe – United Kingdom – England – Cambridgeshire – Cambridge – Business and Economy – Property

Finding things out from electronic sources

Exercise on page 87

'picture AND london AND thames'

Exercise on page 89

1 Enter 'fishing fife tayside' in the box 'with all of the words'.
2 Enter 'fife tayside' in the box 'with at least one of the words'.
3 Enter 'tayside' in the box 'with all of the words' and enter 'dundee' in the box 'without the words'.
4 Enter 'fishing' in the box 'with all of the words' and enter 'fife tayside' in the box 'with at least one of the words'.

Exercise on page 90

When we tried these searches, Search 1 gave lots of references to people-carrier vehicles, but Search 2 was more successful in returning useful websites.

Finding things out from people

Exercise on page 95

1 A local vet
2 Any older person who had been evacuated

3 The secretary of the local pressure group opposing the motorway development

4 The manager of the council leisure centre

Exercise on page 97

1 Expert knowledge
2 Experience
3 Opinions
4 Expert knowledge

Dealing with information

Exercise on page 107

1 Needs to be current
2 Does not need to be current
3 Does not need to be current
4 Needs to be current
5 Needs to be current

Exercise on page 112

The site is maintained by the National Health Service, so the information should be reliable.

Exercise on page 112

1 Primary source
2 Primary source
3 Secondary source
4 Secondary source
5 Primary source
6 Secondary source
7 Primary source
8 Secondary source
9 Primary source
10 Secondary source
11 Primary source

ANSWERS TO EXERCISES

Exercise on page 117

Every one of these activities is illegal. (Although number six, the selling of 'pirate' DVDs, is different from the others as it is being done for commercial purposes.)

Sources of further information

Information on paper
These two websites give useful information on the differences between British English and American English:

http://www.scit.wlv.ac.uk/~jphb/american.html
http://www.pericles.demon.co.uk/amer-eng/index.html

The Ordnance Survey website describes its different products and gives a comprehensive overview of the National Grid at:

http://www.ordnancesurvey.co.uk/oswebsite/

Finding things out from paper sources
This website explains the basics of the Dewey Decimal System:

http://www.usd320.k12.ks.us/whs/lmc/Dewey.html

Information in electronic form
It is possible to use a search engine to find relevant information in blogs. There is an example using the Google search engine at:

http://blogsearch.google.com/blogsearch?hl=en

Dealing with information
Here is a selection of informative websites that will help you to find out more about copyright information:

http://www.patent.gov.uk/copy.htm
http://www.intellectual-property.gov.uk/index.htm
http://www.library.manchester.ac.uk/eresources/copyright/
http://www.abdn.ac.uk/library/copyright.shtml

Index